Magic Bullets in Real Estate

Magic Bullets in Real Estate

Your Complete Guide to Understanding and Using Real Estate to Your Best Advantage

Dan Auito

Hathshire Press
Kodiak, Alaska

Although the author and publisher have made every effort to ensure the accuracy and completeness of information contained in this book, we assume no responsibility for errors, inaccuracies, omissions, or any inconsistency herein. Any slights of people, places, or organizations are unintentional.

First printing 2004

ISBN 0-9740020-0-3
LCCN 2003112265

ATTENTION CORPORATIONS, UNIVERSITIES, COLLEGES, AND PROFESSIONAL ORGANIZATIONS: Quantity discounts are available on bulk purchases of this book for educational, gift purposes, or as premiums for increasing magazine subscriptions or renewals. Special books or book excerpts can also be created to fit specific needs. For information, please contact Hathshire Press, 1619 Three Sisters Way, Kodiak, AK 99615; (907) 481-6300; www.MagicBullets.com.

This book is dedicated to you, the reader. I have written it to protect, educate, encourage, entertain, and enlighten you. This book has power if you apply the basic principles and techniques that are presented. Open up your mind and the opportunities all around you.

Rock the boat and create change for yourself— starting now!

TABLE OF CONTENTS

Part III: Appendices

PREFACE

I wrote this book for my friends and their families as well as their friends and families. To every one of you, I sincerely hope I have answered some of the many questions you have frequently asked. I also hope that I have given you further insights to begin asking more.

What qualifies me to write a book? I believe my sincere desire to help as many people as I can to understand that they can do real estate if they really want or need to is reason enough. My credentials are two real estate licenses, an appraiser's certification, 17 properties of my own, thousands of hours of practical hands-on experience, and 14 years of helping other people as well as myself to better understand and use real estate to live a more fruitful and fulfilling life.

This book is an attempt to answer and give solutions to the many questions I receive daily. I want to help others understand the basics in real estate from the small residential investor's viewpoint. By writing this I hope to assist you in your efforts to develop plans, goals, and objectives in addition to a whole lot more. My intention is to show you how you can use real estate to really secure your financial future and have a great time doing it.

My hope is to interest, protect, and educate you while I organize, support, and expand your awareness. I'll give you tools, strategies, tactics, resources, insights, practical advice, and a multitude of ideas that you can *actually* understand and use immediately to begin achieving your chosen objectives.

I'm going to save you time, trial, error, and frustration while showing you how to find, evaluate, negotiate, contract, rehabilitate, market, and either live in, rent, manage, or sell property. I'll give you all the tricks of the trade I know. I promise not to hold anything back. Some professionals will disagree with me on many points. I'll ask you to use your own judgment and decide for yourself.

In writing this book, I have drawn from my own experience. I haven't relied on law firms, professional companies, or technical writers to infuse the material with highly complicated explanations that can often bore, confuse, and overwhelm the average reader. I have kept it simple! I also provide room at the end of each chapter for you to capture your own ideas while writing down any points or questions you may have that need further research later.

I encourage you from the start to note your thoughts as you read, since typically they are fleeting. By doing this from the beginning, not only will you have a record and a method of using these sections to design your plan at the end of this book, but you also will be able to further clarify and define the specific subjects discussed that I—for fear of losing your attention—did not dwell on to a great extent.

Who can use this book? Certainly the beginning investor. This includes seasoned real estate investors who continuously look for new resources, first-time buyers, people selling by owner, landlords, professional real estate service providers in all fields, and especially blue-collar workers who have decided to move ahead.

It has taken me one year to assemble, document, and present to you 14 years of real-life practical hands-on experience. From years of Internet research to more than a thousand books and/or courses either read or reviewed, I think you will enjoy the results of my efforts to help you better understand and further use the number one wealth generator of all time—real estate—to get ahead in your own life now.

In order to get the most out of this book I simply ask that you keep a positive attitude and be willing to try. In addition, if you will think of how the material can help others as you read then your success will be multiplied. When you take action on your plans and manage your time wisely, you will not be influenced by the dream thieves who tell you all the reasons why something won't work. Simply surround yourself with real estate mentors you trust and continue to read, learn, and try new ideas while taking pride in your work.

I wrote *Magic Bullets in Real Estate* to pass on what I know at this point. If you feel your family or friends could use this book I encourage you to get it to them, since the ultimate Magic Bullet is really in helping other people. Real estate *is* a people business. Enjoy it!

Part I

Overview of the Real Estate Process

Chapter 1

Introduction to the Landscape

In this book, I will show you how to use real estate to your best advantage. By reading and taking notes along the way, you will find that upon finishing the book, a course of action will begin to develop, along with practical steps that will enable you to achieve real results. You will have a concrete plan you can use immediately to start doing real estate now.

Get your highlighter and pencil right now! This book will give you ideas—lots of them. I want you to be able to develop a vision of exactly what part of real estate you need or want to pursue. I don't want to waste your time with philosophical tales of how I or someone else made it in real estate. I want you to get as many original experiences as possible. Capture your thoughts. As soon as you get an "aha" idea, highlight it or write it down before it evaporates so later you can incorporate it into your strategy.

I will begin by getting you to recognize the type of real estate that interests you most. Then I'll show you how to protect yourself from the dangers that may lie ahead. Next, I will give you tools to use along the way while finding the real estate you desire. In addition, you will learn about the power of mentors and how to find and use them. You will be given resource information and a basic education in understanding what creates value. Not only will you learn how to find, negotiate, contract, buy, sell, rehabilitate, and flip properties, but you will discover how to manage tenants, taxes, and tradesmen.

Money and finance play a critical role in real estate, so you will also be given valuable insights into the many financing alternatives that are available to you. You will learn how to buy, sell, and manage your assets without paying commission or management fees. Additionally, you will get ideas and insider tips used by the pros. These will give you a clearer understanding of the following:

● First-time buyer strategies

● How seasoned investors operate

● Rehabilitation of properties

● Home improvement

● Long-term investment planning

● Negotiation basics

● Lending guidelines

● Networking principles

● Positive mental attitude adjustments

Moreover, you'll get a goal-planning outline in a workbook format you can use to get the desired results.

Let's start our journey off by familiarizing you with a few general observations concerning the different types of real estate that may be of interest to you. The sooner you can fix in your mind the specific area or particular type of real estate you will be specializing in, the better you will be able to relate to the rest of the material throughout the book.

The following descriptions are by no means exhaustive. There are many ways to interpret the information and these represent only the tip of the proverbial iceberg. What follows is meant to further assist you in setting your initial sights and then pursuing more in-depth research.

Here are some basic categories of real estate:
- Condominiums, townhomes, and vacation properties
- Single-family homes
- Apartments—residential duplex, triplex, and fourplex
- Commercial—hotels/motels, strip malls, office complexes, mobile home parks, storage units, parking lots, garages, restaurants, stores, apartments with five or more units, etc.
- Industrial—factories, refineries, manufacturing plants, etc.
- Farms—commercial, industrial, or agricultural (depending on zoning)
- Raw land—lots, vacation, recreational, subdividable residential, commercial, industrial, agricultural, and special purpose
- Special purpose—churches, schools, hospitals, power plants, theaters, sports arenas, golf courses, marinas, etc.

There are more classes of property than these, but these are the basics and should get you in the ballpark of what appeals to you now.

Let's look at some of the facets of the individual classes that may be of interest to you upon your further review and understanding below.

● Condominiums, Townhomes, and Vacation Properties

Condominiums and townhomes are very similar. The major difference is that townhomes almost always have two floors, called "split levels." Look for quality construction; good location; ample parking, storage, and amenities; and more square footage. (In the 1970s, people expected 1,500 square feet of living space on average; today, that number has increased to at least 2,000 square feet.) In taller buildings, the top floor corner units with views often are more valuable. Low association fees in well-run, predominantly owner-occupied developments are preferred.

Condos are ideal for second homes, vacation homes, or rentals because of lower purchase price for the same square footage and less building maintenance and yard work. They are often easy to finance.

A note about investing in condominiums: I have seen instances where the local residential housing market for single-family homes becomes so hot, things begin to be sold out or priced out of the reach of the standard homebuyer's price range. The next best thing for these potential buyers is the less expensive condominium. When you see this trend developing, this is the time to go shopping for the best condos you can find since they will soon be in higher demand and will appreciate more quickly. Best are the standard three-bedroom, two-bath configuration that offers what the traditional home normally would.

● Single-Family Homes

Look for mid-priced three-bedroom, two-bath, two-car garage homes (3/2/2) that have large kitchens, baths, and closets with a more open, flowing floor plan. Other considerations are spacious yards, porches, decks, and room for storage. Upgraded components include tile and wood floors; quality fixtures and appliances; solid wood cabinets, doors, and trim; and energy-efficient heating and cooling, double-pane windows, and an overall well-insulated structure.

Always look closely at the plumbing, heating, electrical, roof, foundation, structural integrity, design quality, and location. (Location is so important to real estate you will find it mentioned throughout our discussions.) The safety and quiet of cul-de-sacs are desirable, with corner lots and main streets usually less so in residential housing because of higher taxes, noise, pollution, security concerns, lawn maintenance, and privacy issues. Everyone wants safety, security, and accessability (police, fire, shopping, and quick travel routes) in a home. Homes that face north in the south and south in the north may have some added value for creature comfort.

Overall, single-family homes are the easiest real estate to rent, sell, and finance. They appreciate well, can be used as collateral, and can frequently be purchased below true market value.

● Apartments

For the beginning or small investor, duplex, triplex, and fourplex apartments are the best way to start. They are easier to finance, and they sell more quickly than larger complexes. Operating expenses, such as insurance, trash removal, and so forth, are often less, while at the same time you protect yourself from being 100 percent vacant by having more than one income stream, or source of income, on the property. If you are an owner-occupant, you gain management experience while handling the maintenance on a day-to-day basis.

Median price ranges will appeal to larger segments of the population and will help keep vacancies down. An average building in a nice area is much better than a nice building in a poor area. Larger three-bedroom units have less turnover than the smaller two-bedroom, two-bath or one-bedroom, one-bath efficiency units. They also command higher rents. Proximity to shopping, schools, employment, transportation lines, parks, lakes, rivers, restaurants, and entertainment are most desirable.

Duplexes appreciate faster than triplexes or fourplexes. This is likely because more owners occupy one half, and the added income from the second unit offsets their mortgage obligation and makes it easier for them to qualify for the loan. Thus more demand is created and they rise in value faster. As a short-term buy-and-sell proposition, duplexes hold more immediate profit potential.

Be sure to look for buildings with separate meters for each unit's utilities. Check that the building conforms to local zoning ordinances and classifications. When considering multiple unit dwellings, the R1 designator indicates residential single-family dwellings; R2 indicates low-density multiple dwellings permitted; and R4 indicates high-density residential apartments are permitted. Check with planning and zoning to ensure compliance before committing yourself. Add the following contract clause if you are unsure about zoning: *This offer is contingent upon local zoning ordinances allowing for current use.*

● Commercial

A good multiple-use building should have adequate lighting, durable fixtures, and security; attractive public areas, landscaping, and ample parking; an adequate number of restrooms and meeting and break rooms; efficient heating, cooling, and electrical; and phone, fax, and computer lines. It should be located in close proximity to other complimentary service centers. Commercial property, in general, will benefit from having a high traffic count and being close to large population centers.

Mixed-use commercial properties can be a combination of shopping centers with offices and apartments above, or they can be professional office complexes with doctors, lawyers, CPAs, and agency satellite offices all under one roof. Clinics, food, and personal product centers tend to be somewhat recession-proof so you may look at providing centers of these types.

Further analysis will be required to evaluate operating costs, land use restrictions, location and characteristics concerning growth, travel distances, external appearances, competition, and enough of a population base to support the property.

Note that high-rise buildings are usually financed by or with corporate stock, partnerships, co-operations, syndications, limited liability corporations (LLCs), real estate investment trusts (REITs), insurance companies, pension fund managers, and a host of other large-source-of-capital providers.

● Industrial

Industrial properties often require that airports, railways, highways, and water routes be available to receive raw materials for production and to deliver the finished products when ordered. Frequently, the buildings themselves are large and square with office spaces, loading facilities, heavy-load floor capacities, high usage power supplies, tall ceilings, long structural spans, sprinkler systems, and flat land surfaces for ease of mobility. Buildings suitable for light manufacturing and processing have the greatest appeal since tenants can be tough to find for single-use properties.

You may also want to look at acquiring excess or reserve land area for storage, parking, and future growth potentials.

Keep in mind that industrial property has more potential risks regarding environmental hazards—buried tanks, asbestos, polychlorinated biphenyls (PCBs), cesspools, ponds, pits, drums, dead vegetation, protruding pipes, odors, burying, burning, dump sites, lead, radon, and contamination in general. Don't buy an Environmental Protection Agency nightmare, since you could be responsible for cleanup costs!

Beginners should consider small industrial park properties as a safe way to enter this field of investment. If you want to be a king (or queen!) of industry, you'll need further education on finance, negotiation, and cash-flow analysis.

● Raw Land

Raw land includes residential, commercial, industrial, agricultural, and special purpose. It is often referred to as an "alligator" because it always wants to be fed—cash—but provides no immediate benefits. Raw land is cash intensive because it usually does not generate adequate rental income to cover its carrying costs. Subdividing and buying in the way of growth, however, can make it a very profitable investment. Look at proposed roads and sewer systems that lead to farmlands and undeveloped land that could be rezoned to higher and better uses in the near future.

Prospective buyers usually look for views, location, potable water, good drainage and topography, access to roads, feasible sewer and utility connections, and road frontage with corner lots that double visibility for commercial applications. If you're looking for agricultural use, you may search for timber and mineral rights. Lakes, rivers, streams, and wildlife might be important for land to be used for recreation. Research easements, zoning restrictions, and ordinances, as well as covenants and deed restrictions relating to your intended purposes—especially if you are planning on subdividing the property now or in the future—are desirable. (See Appendix F: "Bonus Report: Getting Raw Land—Not a Raw Deal!" for information concerning raw land.)

● Special Purpose

Churches, theaters, hospitals, schools, sports arenas, golf courses, old firehouses, railroad stations, marinas, silos, mills, bunkers, and so forth, These are often great candidates for conversion to other more profitable uses. Don't rule them out!

● Location

Location, location, and location, as they say, are the three most important things in real estate. With residential property, that boils down to safety, security, and convenience. You might get a great deal on a piece of property but if it takes you a half hour to get a loaf of bread, what kind of resale will you get? Another good deal may back up to or face a busy street. That's often a poor choice as well—noise, pollution, the loss of privacy, and curb appeal are all factors.

Do you know who the largest commercial real estate owner in the United States is? It's the McDonald's Corporation. On top of that, they also have the most valuable locations for their type of business. The research they do on demographics and traffic counts is unparalleled.

If you were ever going to open a fast-food restaurant, just put it near a McDonald's. You would survive just on the volume of people who pass by the location McDonald's has already decided meets all the critical data to support their restaurant business. Your restaurant, if you had good food and service, would flourish. Just sell something a little different than McDonald's.

That's leveraging someone else's expertise in evaluating a location for a certain type of real estate.

This is the principle of using proven research—that is, using other people's proven research to ensure a desired result. By studying fundamental truths and motivating forces, mega-corporations discover and implement natural methods of operation. Other people's proven research and principles are like natural laws. A natural law works in every situation in its own way. It's like gravity—it always works! (Here on earth, anyway.)

In real estate it doesn't matter what type it is—commercial, residential, industrial, or recreational. Look for signs that serious market studies have been undertaken by major operators and buy things that can flourish in the presence of those concerns.

For instance, let's use Home Depot as an example. If Home Depot decides to build on a site, every residential lot within a mile of that new center will be bought up as soon as the Home Depot commits to build. Why? Because smart investors know that Home Depot has done the market study and the area will become prosperous.

On top of that, it will provide jobs, it will pay taxes, it will provide materials with which to build the neighborhoods, and people will shop there once their houses are built. The same goes for Wal-Mart, Lowe's, and other smart business concerns.

You may or may not have noticed this but take a look the next time you are driving around. As you drive into cities from the suburbs, you'll notice donut shops, gas stations with convenience coffee centers, bagel shops, and so forth, on the side of the road people travel on their way into the city to go to work. These are morning activity business centers.

On your way home, out of the city, you will see restaurants that cater to the evening meal crowd: KFC, Taco Bell, Subway, and Pizza Hut. That's because people don't go there for breakfast. They shop there on their way home, outbound from the city at night. If you put your restaurant on the wrong side of the road, you could be making a huge strategical error. Think!

● Finding the Right Property

The best type of real estate to buy is *property no one else knows is for sale.* Why? Because there is no competition.

The other best property to buy is *property no one else wants.* Why might no one want the property? There are many reasons for this, including:

- Inability to look past serious cosmetic distress
- Misconceptions or lack of ability to repair existing defects— termites, foundation problems, rotten trusses, and so forth
- Stigmatized property because of death, divorce, or some other unfortunate circumstance
- Fear of surrounding neighborhood conditions
- Legal issues such as local, state, or federal liens on the property (clouds on the title)

If you can overcome whatever created those negative attitudes concerning a particular property, you often will make a considerable amount of money for your time and effort. You can often find jewels in places that seem hopeless. In real estate *you make money when you solve problems.* For instance, the following are some pluses to accepting property others can't seem to tackle:

- Lower price because of low demand or appeal
- Higher profits because of legal rather than material defects
- Changing market conditions could lead to higher resale values
- Investment properties can be looked at unemotionally
- Cost of repairs and estimated time can be assessed more quickly than by the average, uneducated buyer

Foreclosures can also be profitable, but I urge you to be cautious. They are often highly publicized, so you will likely have plenty of competition. Don't overbid in the frenzy of an auction. Know what you are willing to pay and not a penny more. Watch out for shills and sophisticated investors; don't get burned.

When looking for property, be sure you know with whom you are dealing. My advice to a first-time buyer is to *try to buy real estate from people who don't know much about real estate but are also genuinely motivated to sell for obvious reasons.* Look for a sense of urgency on the seller's part; this will give you the edge in negotiation. If they know the lingo and terminology of the trade then you have an idea that you are dealing with a potentially well-educated seller who may get the better end of the deal. Don't get burned, tricked, or conned into paying more than the property's true value.

If you really like a shrewd seller's property, be sure to do your research as to value, terms, and conditions. Investigate who will pay for certain closing costs, inspections, and repairs. Once you are satisfied, then make your best offer and walk away. (Of course, the entire agreement should be subject to your attorney's approval!)

You may never need a real estate agent, but a good real estate attorney and title company are absolute musts anytime you are going to contract on anything. Do yourself a huge favor early in your career and insert into all of your agreements the following statement: *This entire agreement is subject to my attorney's approval.* Have the other party sign and date that statement and follow through and get your attorney to review the entire agreement. This is your legal escape clause. It is the safety valve in high-stakes negotiation. Use it.

These liability-limiting statements can cover you in the case of fleas, ticks, and parasites who will try anything to take advantage of honest, caring, and hardworking people to get a free ride.

While on the subject of the legal issues involved with just about everything in life, I will also put my own disclaimer here if for no other reason than to show you how they work: *The information in this book is not intended to be a substitute for any legal advice. If you have any doubts or questions, I advise you to consult an attorney.*

A note on attorneys: They are trained to be problem finders, not deal approvers, so they will often find a lot of minor problems. Make it clear to them that you want protection from major boo-boos and you can live with things that are harmless to you even though they are present. Don't let your lawyer kill your deal without a good reason.

Another reason to consult your attorney is to discuss how you should operate. I know of many real estate investors who have incorporated their businesses under the protection of a limited liability corporation (LLC). Trusts also protect real estate interests.

● ● ● ● CAPTURED IDEAS ● ● ● ●

This section occurs at the end of each chapter. I hope you will learn something of value from what you've read that will help you reach your goals.

Notes—*insights, ideas, actions to take*

_____

_____

_____

Strategy—*planning for success*

_____

_____

_____

Tactics—*ways to achieve success*

_____

_____

_____

Chapter 2

Never Pay Rent Again— A Primer to Homeownership

If you are just getting started, I encourage you to buy your own home first. You will get better interest rates, and there are lower initial down-payment requirements. You also will get a practical, hands-on education immediately by closing on your first deal.

Do you think you cannot afford a place of your own? I must respectfully disagree. Although some people are resigned to the thought they can never afford a home of their own, this does not have to be. In truth, nearly anyone who wants it bad enough can buy a home of their own. With that thought in mind, I believe the very best way to approach or begin to take steps toward homeownership is to start getting organized!

● Getting Organized

The first step in getting organized is to take an inventory of what you have working for and against you. I suggest you start with finance. Here is where you consider every credit card you own and loan you have that currently has a balance you are obligated to pay.

This is hands-on credit consolidation; you personally do it all. Total up the dollar amount you currently owe to everyone and find the credit card or loan that is charging you the highest interest rate. Once you have zeroed in on the lender charging the highest interest rate, make it your mission to pay it off first. You will be diverting all other available cash to reduce this high interest lender's hold on you to *zero*.

You should use as much available lower interest rate money to shift the balances of the much higher interest debt to the lower interest charge cards' rate. Use the balance transfer checks to pay off the highest interest-charging bad guys first.

Tip: Use any pre-approved cards that tease you with no interest for one year or more to transfer balances and pay no interest while you eliminate your debt.

In order to quickly pay off the highest interest rate lender first, pay only the minimum required monthly payment to all the lower interest rate loans, and take every diverted extra dollar that is available for debt reduction and put it toward paying the high card or loan off first. Once that card is paid off, call the company and close that account. Celebrate by cutting that card up into small pieces. Have a little ceremony that symbolizes the death of bad debt!

Now continue doing that same thing—putting all available money toward your next highest interest rate credit card or loan, only now, add to it everything that you were paying toward the first card that is now gone. You will find that your debts will be paid off more quickly because more money is being freed up to pay the next lender in line. In debt shifting I call this "putting the hammer down" because you will be pounding these lenders with larger and larger amounts at faster and faster rates with every card and loan you retire and close out!

Keep using the above technique until all your debts are paid!

The second step is to put into place a needed spending freeze—literally. Put all your credit cards in a bag of water and put them in the freezer. Inform everyone that every discretionary dollar needs to pass a unanimous decision in order to be spent. That means no knickknacks or doodads. Everyone is expected to tighten up their spending habits and use only cash.

Plastic is like play money; it is easy to use. Stop falling into the lender's trap of fooling you into believing that you're not spending real money—you are! Pay cash and you will pay attention.

There are many ways to restructure debt. Let's look at a few. If you are driving a new car, sell it and get out from underneath those high payments. Drive something less expensive while you eliminate debt and prepare to qualify to buy your own home. Start staying home on Friday and Saturday nights. Eating out is expensive and it adds up fast. Do your own cooking at home for much lower cost meals. Limit your entertainment expenses.

The third step is to start finding ways to *make more money as well as save it.* There are a number of ways to do this as well. If you punch a time clock, start getting in a few more hours. Tell the boss you're buckling down. If you can manage a second job, or a better one, take it. Unload all your junk by having a yard sale. If you can downsize or share rent with someone else for a while, do it! Now apply all that extra cash you have right on top of that highest interest rate card or loan.

So organize an effort to, in effect, get organized. The only way things change is by making a commitment to start, one step at a time. Once your budget is established, all you have to do is adjust it, fine-tune it, and stick with it.

The next extreme act of intelligent financial wisdom you can use is to schedule a day when you can attend a free homebuyer's workshop. Just read the real estate section of your local Sunday paper or contact your local housing commission. These sources will tell you where and when these free classes are held. Commit to go! Put the date on your calendar and make arrangements for your partner to attend if you have one. It's a day-long event that will help you enormously.

While at the homebuyer's class, you will be shown how to use grants, first-time homebuyer programs, low interest loans, no money down programs, and forgivable loans where you don't have to repay them after a certain period of time. You will be amazed at how easy it can be to get into a home of your own, especially if you are a low-income, first-time buyer. If you can show that you have a job and your debts are manageable and you really want a home of your own, odds are good that you will end up having it. (Note: Most lenders consider your status to be "first time" if you haven't owned your own home within the last three years.)

The homebuyer programs open the door to homeownership. They will explain it all to you along with other people who will be learning and preparing to take advantage of all the opportunity these great local, state, and federal programs represent. I still attend them when I have the chance—even after buying 17 of my own properties.

It's all about being informed, organized, and determined to do it. Start today by gathering up all of your financial information and organizing your bill paying plan to nail just that one highest interest rate card first. That's a doable step, so take it.

If you feel that you cannot restructure your debt by doing what I suggest, contact a nonprofit consumer credit counseling service. They can propose to you a plan that will work for your specific situation and needs.

A good friend of mine puts it this way: When people are feeling sorry for themselves and in some twisted way continue to feel sorry for themselves while choosing not to change the things they have power over, they are in essence sitting on the fur-lined pity pot having their own private pity party. That creates a hopeless case of desperation that accomplishes nothing. So get off the pot and *get into action*. This will cure your fears and change your life. The minute you decide to fight, invisible forces start to align to help you begin to live on purpose. My purpose is to show you how you can join the ranks of proud homeowners. I want to see you succeed.

Don't shrug off what I have just said as being intended for someone else; it is meant for you! It works for people who want it to.

Get motivated, find something that is bigger than you are, and work toward it. That's what has given me the inner drive to believe I could write a book that will help other people enjoy their lives just a little bit more.

● A Military Strategy

In this section, I hope to spare our military members from the agonizing decision of whether to put their lives on hold for one more tour or to go ahead and take the plunge into homeownership. As a result of speaking to countless military members whom I find kicking themselves while grimacing at the realization of blown opportunities, I would like to offer those brave souls an alternative method for getting hold of the American dream. For the civilian population who will only be staying in one certain location for the short term of three to five years, then this method will work for you as well.

The issue at hand is whether buying real estate and having to sell it within three to five years would in fact provide enough time to recoup and actually make a profit. Will you be relatively comfortable in the knowledge that you can make a fair profit for taking this supposed risk?

For the above reasons I would like to slant this segment toward the military, as it really can help nail down some important concepts for our 3.2 million military members and their families. This strategy can certainly be used by everyone. However, our military members can really maximize this strategy as they often are moved an average of five times throughout a 20-year career.

Let's kick off our story's scenarios, insights, and strategies by emphasizing the sooner you begin to buy real estate, the better your odds will be of accumulating more assets, equity, tax advantages, and wealth. Granted most of you will be civilian but don't count yourself out, since the national average says that most people tend to move every five years. Yes, that's an average, so between grandparents who have lived in the same home for 50 years and the young and mobile moving annually, we actually find that 20 percent of the general population will be on the move each year.

The above fact alone can be a comfort in itself as it says that a fair percentage of people will constantly be in the market to either buy or sell real estate. July 4th weekend is traditionally the hottest home sales period of the year, so with that in mind you'll want to really turn on the sales program to get those bidding wars started. The national averages tend to fluctuate; however, a fair figure to use regarding occupancy per household can be, for our purposes, 2.5 persons per household. I know you're asking how you can have half a person living in a home. Remember, it is the result of averaging—two in one, three in another, resulting in 2.5.

Using a city of 1,000,000 people divided by 2.5 people per household would equal 400,000 housing units. Dividing that by 5 gives us the 20 percent average of homes that will be experiencing new occupants due to people moving; 20 percent of 400,000 equals 80,000 units available. Now we can further adjust our estimates using census data that says 28 percent of the population lives in rented housing, which leaves us with the pseudo-figure of 72 percent or 57,600 homes that will most likely be bought and sold in that year.

Using all the weird science above we can simplify this and say that for every 100 dwellings existing, 400,000 divided by 57,600 equals 6.94 houses per hundred that will be put on the market annually for sale. You could also divide that 57,600 by 365 days of the year and say that on average 158 homes are being bought or sold per day in that city. Remember, though, that spring and summer are the hot-selling months and the majority of homes will sell within the five best selling months: May, June, July, August, and September. What does all this information tell us? I believe it justifies our reasons to buy, as you can well see that a market does exist on a continual basis and when we have a clear idea on how to operate in that environment, we can capitalize on it by having a plan!

So what's the plan? I have executed the following plan many times and have also encouraged and facilitated many more for individuals who were at first confused, hesitant, and to varying degrees, uninformed. Here is one plan that I know works, so we won't be guessing on this one!

The first thing that you need to do is make up your mind that upon arrival to your new location, you will not rent or accept subsidized housing. Once you've decided that buying is the way to go, then determine what type of real estate will satisfy your family's needs. The standard and most sought-after housing product is the traditional three-bedroom, two-bath, and two-car garage home. If you can afford it, then you should, at the very least, consider it; the main reason is it will sell faster when you decide that it is time to sell!

Beware! You may have competition in finding these hot properties but don't get discouraged. Keep hunting until yours turns up because you will build in a measure of safety by having that same in-demand property when it comes time to sell. Another key element is to visit or contact a local lender in the community in which you will be buying, in order to get prequalified for a certain loan amount *before* you go house hunting. This is a virtually free service that lenders perform in order to determine how much house you can afford. By getting prequalified (and having your preapproval letter in hand when you make the offer), the sellers will take you seriously since they'll know you can afford the property and are ready to move fast.

In the armed forces, the service member is often offered base housing instead of a pay increase in the form of BAH (basic allowance for housing) that would otherwise be used to sustain housing off base. Pay scales are uniform throughout the branches of service; however, housing allowances vary according to local costs associated with housing. On average, an E-5 petty officer or sergeant will receive around $1,000 extra a month (tax-free) if they choose to buy instead of going into base housing. That $1,000 a month often qualifies people to be able to afford a house in the range of $150,000.

The same goes for civilians. Why throw that money away on rent or lost entitlements when you could be using it to create equity, tax advantages, and appreciation? On top of that, service members automatically qualify for a Veterans Administration Loan (VA) guarantee, which means they can buy with virtually no money down! Civilians can get 3 to 5 percent down loans in many cases. Note: VA funding fee equals 2.2 percent of the loan, no PMI required.

By making up your mind to buy upon arrival to a new location, you maximize the time you have to look for, buy, remodel, and sell the home in the dreaded three-to-five-year time period. If you buy under market price and methodically rehabilitate the home while you live there, history tells us that an adequate profit is often the result when you sell it. Paint, carpet, tile, landscaping, fences, sheds, shelving, wallpaper, new faucets, cabinets, and vanities can indeed make your home worth considerably more than you paid for it.

Don't forget that an average inflation rate of 3 percent compounded over three years will add $13,909.05 to your home's value alone, making it worth $163,909 if you did no improvements and just maintained it in good order. Let's also remember that you may have bought a three-bedroom, two-bath, two-car garage home under market value and your mortgage has been paid down a little, while at the same time you have been methodically improving the property with the intent to sell it for top dollar at the peak of the feeding frenzy in early July. Come on gang, this ought to be illegal—with me telling you how it's done, you're going to have a huge advantage over the folks who don't have this strategy!

Remember to buy in good neighborhoods to protect your values. You also want to buy homes with sound plumbing, electrical, and heating; solid foundations; structural integrity; and a solid roof in desirable locations, at below market rates. This puts you in a cosmetic "rehab," not the classic money pit. You want real estate that needs cosmetics, not expensive hidden defects that call for a repairman. Go to www.InspectAmerica.com for free inspection sheets.

The icing on the cake is to sell the home "by owner" when the time comes. Here are a few quick basics on how to do it successfully on your own. First, since you have all this great information that I'm giving you, you will be well positioned to do this. If you get confused, pay a trusted real estate professional for just the specific service that you need, and not on a percentage fee but using a flat fee. The industry is headed in that direction already.

Here's the brief: You bought the house as soon as you could in the best area at the best price, with minimal major repairs needed. Over a three-to-five-year period, you methodically rehabilitated it with paint, carpet/floor coverings, landscaping, fencing, vanities, faucets, etc. You know that you are doing these repairs and improvements with the intent to sell, so you have used neutral colors and earth tones that generally everyone likes. Now your home should show very well when people come to see it, so your preparation is almost done. By organizing the details of your sale up to six months in advance, you can wait for your higher sale price. You won't be in a rush and you won't have to discount your price in order to move on to your next destination.

Here are two very simple rules in selling any home:

1. Price it right; get your own appraisal before you advertise it for sale.

2. Advertise it properly, widely, and often, via newspapers, Internet, bulletin boards, word of mouth, yard signs, corner signs, open houses, brochures, fact sheets, flyers, etc.

Now keep the house sparkling clean. Box up all clutter and stack the boxes neatly down the center of the garage. Clear out closets, remove framed photos from the walls, and get rid of old furniture in a moving sale, which you should organize a couple of months before you move. Note: Let moving sale attendees know your home will be for sale soon!

Not everyone will attempt to sell "by owner"; the percentages are small, so my fellow real estate agents really have no reason to be upset here. If you will use a real estate attorney to handle your sales contracts and related disclosure documents, you can usually have the whole thing done for about $750. On a sale like the one we have been talking about here, you may also offer the same deal to a real estate agent to see if they would be willing to match the attorney's price. By using an attorney, a title company, staying in contact with lenders, and getting your own home inspection and appraisal beforehand, you will find that your sale will go smoother than you might have thought possible. A $10,000 commission can be saved if you're willing to do the work by preparing in these proficient ways.

At this point you need to have a little faith; you're smarter than the majority of homeowners. After all, you have had a plan since you bought the home. Believe me when I say that you will do an excellent job in selling this home and when you do, you will pay no capital gains on your profit unless you have already exceeded your individual lifetime capital gains deduction of $250,000, or $500,000 for married couples.

I must confess I feel as though I've been conservative on the profit potential, since I have consistently averaged an approximate $30,000 profit on most deals. If you repeat this process over twenty years and you move five times, $30,000 multiplied by five moves equals $150,000. When you sell that last house you can take the money with you and retire back home, and buy a $150,000 retirement home free and clear, thereby in the end, having Uncle Sam buy you a house instead of renting one for you! One final note: Because of a moderate 3 percent inflation rate compounding over those 20 years, the same $150,000 dollar home today will cost $278,807.35 20 years from now. That's another reason to start buying today: Real estate is considered an inflation hedge.

For the people who chose to rent or live in base housing for those twenty years, it is an unfortunate loss of opportunity, since they don't get the equivalent of a free house. *You will* if you begin to take steps now toward buying your homes using better methods, plans, and strategies to achieve your long-term goals.

Don't wait! The concept works—*if* you work it!

● ● ● ● CAPTURED IDEAS ● ● ● ●

Notes—*insights, ideas, actions to take*

_____

_____

_____

_____

_____

_____

Strategy—*planning for success*

_____

_____

_____

_____

_____

Tactics—*ways to achieve success*

_____

_____

_____

_____

_____

_____

Chapter 3

Building Your Resources, Planning Your Strategy

Now that you have an idea what type of property you might be looking for, here are some ideas, strategies, and tactics to find those deals.

You need to define your strategy. What is it going to be? Buying your first home, selling your existing home, high rises, duplexes, triplexes, lease purchases with options to buy, owner-financed deals, single-family homes, trailer parks, commercial, residential, and/or industrial. Choose something you love because your work will be pleasurable and you will become very good at it. Once you feel confident at your craft, you then will be called upon to use your skill in helping others to enjoy their lives better through your abilities to guide them. This is what I am attempting to do for you.

Let's go over some definitions.

- *Strategy:* The artful means of planning, directing, and maneuvering yourself into a position to take advantage of what real estate has to offer. I am going to ask you to define your goals later on after I have given you those ideas I keep talking about.

- *Tactics:* The specific things you use to reach your goal, the methods, the diplomacy, skill, and care of execution in all that you undertake to achieve your real estate objectives.

● *Tools and preparation:* Get a map, preferably what is called a street finder, which you can buy at your local bookstore. This is an invaluable time-saving tool. You get pinpoint accuracy to the address you seek and you get an overview of the neighborhood in general as you look at the area's grid.

● *Cell phone:* Great deals go fast. You must be available when the hot tip comes in. Get a cell phone and publicize that number. A beeper is cheaper, but less effective.

● *Marketing:* You may think you are just a little old real estate investor, but in reality you are going to have to be a master advertising specialist. Your objective is to inform your entire community that you are in the business of buying and/or selling real estate, and solving problems. Get your business cards printed with this in mind.

Look the part; be business-like and present an appearance that says, "I am capable of helping you achieve your objective." Drive a reliable car and be well groomed.

If you can, get your financing options in order. Yes, you can buy real estate with nothing down; however, you will go much further, much faster if you use OPM, or *other people's money.* This means the bank. The better your credit, the easier you will find real estate investing to be. Ask a lender to preapprove you.

If you know of someone who has substantial cash reserves in a bank earning 3 percent interest, you could offer him or her 7 percent to use the money to buy real estate. This person's money would be safe since the home would serve as collateral. Buy the house, fix it up, sell it for a profit, and pay off your 7 percent loan—and you keep the profit. Build your cash reserves by doing this over and over again.

Next—and before going all out on a property acquisition blitz—do a little homework. It's waiting for you at your local bookstore. Whether you hit your favorite independent store with its knowledgeable staff or the mega-store with its big selection, be prepared to spend some time looking through real estate titles. You will almost automatically gravitate to the books that interest you and that is a key to your success. You must remain motivated and excited and be driven to learn and expand your horizons by applying that to the real world of real estate investment.

I probably have at least 100 real estate books in my personal collection, not to mention textbooks from various courses I've taken. I have always found at least one idea in each book that pays me back tenfold. I spend some time at the bookstore looking at title after title, and I am always able to find a book or two that really nails down what I want to know on a certain subject.

I recommend you not go to the library for the following reasons: (1) the material can be outdated, (2) you have to return the book, and (3) you can't write in the book, takes notes, or highlight passages for reference later. Start building your collection immediately, since you will find yourself searching for ideas and information on a regular basis.

While I am on the subject, here is a big no-no: Never loan your books out or give them to other people. Too frequently, people don't return them and you will probably forget who you loaned it to. Don't loan your real estate books. Period.

I recommend you have the following books in your collection:

- The street finder map book, local edition
- A real estate dictionary
- A real estate tax book (most recent edition since tax law changes)
- A homebuyer's inspection guide with checklists
- *The Landlording Manual* by Leigh Robinson, if you will be in rental property
- *The Realty Bluebook* by Robert de Heer—very comprehensive
- One or two additional books that jump out at your innate interests

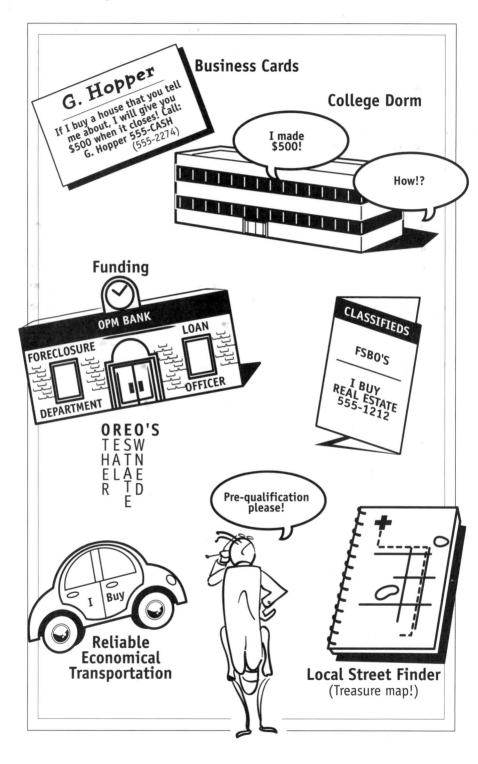

Be sure to visit www.audrie.com for legal forms, www.realtor.com for real estate searches, and www.mrlandlord.com for questions and answers, plus a lot more.

I can't emphasize enough that you start noting ideas as they come to you so you can get the best result out of reading, thinking, and applying those insights along the way. In this book, put a star next to paragraphs that were the triggers of thought, then go back and review them later. Fill in the blanks that are provided below. Did you get at least one idea yet? You will find sections throughout the text that ask you to stop and think about what you have just finished reading. Part of the process of designing plans is to capture potential ideas and insights along the way. By making notes along the way you will be able to keep your mind on the next section without that gnawing feeling in the back of your mind that can distract you from focusing on the current topic being discussed.

Start a personal address book for all your real estate contacts—and I do mean all of them—including your tenants. The following is a rundown of specialties in order, as you may need them.

Fill in the blanks. You need these people:

	What they do	Who they are	Phone number	Email address
Attorney				
Commercial banker				
Mortgage broker				
Home inspector				
Appraiser				
Title company				
Surveyor				
Insurance agent				
Pest control company				
Real estate buyer's agent				
Rental manager				
Home warranty company				
Moving company				
Home security company				
Electrician				
Plumber				
Heating and cooling company				
Roofing company				
Skilled carpenter				
Flooring company and installer				
Painter				
Appliance repair				
Landscape maintenance company				
Cleaning service				
Tax planning (CPA)				
Tenants				

This is your short list. By getting the names and numbers of city officials, utility department heads, planning and zoning officials, code inspectors, the county recorder's office, the sheriff, fire marshal, various lenders, leaders, and a host of others, you can have quick access to a large network of support personnel and be on a first name basis when you place those all-important calls. (Hint: Get private numbers and promise not to give them out! This will save time.)

All of the above people can be any of these: information resources, bounty hunters, assistants, educators, specialists, networkers, referrals, facilitators, strategists, tacticians, problem solvers, buyers, sellers, partners, friends, or tenants.

As I have said before, real estate is a people business. Start out on the right foot and acquire and organize your network of professionals. I call them my "A Team." Give all of these people your cards and employ them as bird dogs, or bounty hunters. Pay them for referrals but more importantly, use them exclusively when you need their particular specialty. Also, refer them often to people who you find need their assistance. Loyalty to others will get you special preferential treatment and in this industry, that is a very valuable tool in your toolbox.

● Moving Up—or Out

After you have lived in your own home for a year, you should have improved it considerably. Get a new appraisal, which will likely result in a higher valuation. When you have that higher value, set up an equity line as a primary residence line of credit.

Now go hunting for your next larger home. Remember to buy it right and build in value when you buy below market. Once you find it, start the rental ball rolling on your first house and find good tenants. Follow my instructions from Chapter 11 on how landlords can learn to read minds, and it should be trouble-free for you.

Please let me save all the people who have a spouse or significant other a lot of headaches early on. Eventually, you are going to want to stay put. You don't want to keep moving every time you buy another property so give yourself and your family some stability. Learn to buy property without having to move into each of them. Use equity lines, owner financing, or 20 percent down investor rates for nonowner-occupied loans, leases with options to buy, and so forth. (By going to websites such as www.Lease2Purchase.com, you can learn how to use lease options in many ways. The subject is an entire book in itself!)

Keep business and pleasure separate. Your home should be a sanctuary. All the money in the world is worthless if your home life is in shambles. Balance is required, and it should be part of your overall strategy.

● ● ● ● CAPTURED IDEAS ● ● ● ●

Notes—*insights, ideas, actions to take*

_____

_____

_____

_____

Strategy—*planning for success*

_____

_____

_____

Tactics—*ways to achieve success*

_____

_____

_____

_____

Chapter 4
Using Mentors as Your Guides

I highly recommend you jump-start your education and go tell a friendly experienced investor the whole truth and nothing but the truth. Let him or her know you are new—he or she will know anyway—and ask for help. Try to repay this person in any appropriate way possible. What you are after is any and all of their materials, forms, techniques, strategies, knowledge, and contacts in the local area. These individuals have connections and real estate is a people business. You need to get hooked into the network of power players as soon as you can. This way you have a greater chance of success and less chance of getting burned and disenchanted.

By attending local real estate investor and/or apartment owner meetings or seminars, you will come into contact with some very educated people. Not only will you learn a great deal about real estate, but you will also meet people who are willing to help or guide you. Find someone you like and get along with and ask him or her for assistance.

You should ask questions of a potential mentor, then sit back, be quiet, and let him or her speak. Your job is to listen and only speak to further clarify your understanding. This is exercising the potential mentor's mental reflex of recall. From here, you tap the fountain of knowledge and experience. Questions control conversations. Ask, then listen!

Everyone can mentor you in some way. When you sincerely ask people to pass on to you their expertise, you validate them as valuable human beings. Psychological air is what circulates in the atmosphere of human understanding. You're listening and you're learning. They are reliving the success of prior triumph.

Mentors tend to be centers of influence. They can inform, support, advise, and refer. They have knowledge, contacts, resources, experience, and ability. These people have *power*. When you plug into this source, you can become energized with high levels of enthusiasm, renewed motivation, and inner drive.

That scenario creates momentum, which creates energy, which expands your world. Now honor the person who has given you a piece of him- or herself and redistribute a piece of yourself. You add value to people's lives when you pass it on. You relate better.

You must first seek to understand and then be understood. Too many people want to talk and appear to be an expert. Ask direct, hard-hitting questions that require intelligence to answer. Are there any pearls of wisdom to be gained? Can your store of knowledge be increased or is it plain to see that your energy is being depleted?

What else generates power for us? What about books, practice, and trial and error? Even failure is a great teacher. Power is gained by helping others. This is offering power and in return, getting more—a Magic Bullet!

● Finding a Real Estate Professional

If you decide you want to enlist the help of a real estate professional, read this section first.

Most books encourage you to use full-time agents who are dedicated to their profession—those who do it day in and day out, who depend on the business to put bread on the table. This is good advice. You will most often get a highly competent professional who will see to the details and accomplish the mission for you.

Because I care about you and your success, I want to give you my spin on the subject.

I am a part-time agent. I am also dedicated. I went to schools and through the tests to acquire the education for my own learning benefit and to increase my understanding of the subject from the inside out. My *real* education has come through helping others to achieve their goals. As they say, you must truly understand a subject before you can teach it. If you doubt this, try it!

Based on my experience, some full-time agents hold back on various phases of the real estate process. They don't take the time to educate or create a complete understanding of the process and opportunities involved in real estate matters. I believe the reason for this is they just don't have the time. They are there to facilitate a transaction—and then another and another. Their kids just keep eating and they need the income. Can you blame them?

Here's a brief explanation of agency relationships:

● An *agent* is a person entrusted with another's business, an agent is authorized to represent and act for his or her principal client. A salesperson who is either an employee or an independent contractor is the agent of his or her broker as well.

● *Single agency* exists when a seller or buyer is represented by a broker or his or her agent. In this relationship the broker owes the duties of fairness and honesty, the broker must present all offers unless told otherwise by his client, the broker must maintain confidentiality while obeying lawful orders. The broker must remain loyal and disclose all material facts that affect his or her client's interests, must account for all funds, and must use skill, care, and diligence throughout the transaction. In single agency it is buyer or seller not both.

● *Dual agency* can come into play when a broker lists a property with his or her client and also finds and brings a buyer's offer to his seller. In this case the broker must ask permission from his principal client to transition to the status of transaction broker by getting the written consent of his or her client seller before doing so. This allows the sale to proceed but the responsibilities are now limited to honest and fair dealing, accounting for all funds and continued use of skill, care, and diligence in the transaction.

● *Transaction broker* is a broker who provides limited representation to a buyer, seller, or both in a real estate transaction, but does not represent either in a fiduciary capacity or as a single agent. The transaction broker is there to effect the smooth transfer of real estate between members of the public whom they do not strictly represent by a brokerage relationship contract. Some states are mandating this type of agency be the sole method of employment of brokerage firms. Check with your prospective agent regarding agency.

Don't let all this confuse you; simply ensure that the brokerage you choose to deal with explains the details in plain language while presenting the paperwork necessary to get the deal done.

If you decide you do want a full-time real estate pro to guide you, look for the following characteristics in the individual you choose:

● They should know the mechanics of how to structure and carry out all the details of a real estate transaction.

● They should be available for you. You should be able to reach them when you have a question.

● Are they willing to mentor you? Will they give you the secrets and tell you everything they know in order to help you? Will they take their time to look at your circumstances and put their life's experiences and knowledge to work for you, then offer you the best option that dovetails with your objectives?

Ask them the following questions:
- Are you a full-time agent? If not, why?
- Do you use assistants?
- What is your real estate specialty?
- May I see your marketing plan?
- How often do you attend board meetings?
- How many buyers do you talk to weekly?
- Will you create a professional flyer for my home?
- Do you have a mission statement?
- How often will you contact me once I list with you?
- How will you update me with the progress of your sales efforts?
- How do you find buyers?
- What marketing techniques will you use?
- How do you tell other agents about my property?
- What can I do to help?
- What are my odds of selling at a certain price?
- How many current listings do you have and what is the average marketing time?
- What will you do specifically to sell my property?

By asking agents these questions, you can learn a lot. Don't be afraid to ask for further clarification on points that you don't quite understand; you need to have a clear understanding on how the process will be going. This will save you and the agent from many hard feelings later as the process goes into the action stage.

Another critical component to success is a well-defined marketing plan that states what will be done to effectively present your home to the buying public. What follows is a marketing checklist; not all approaches are required, but you should review them with your prospective agent to ensure superior representation:

❑ Help you prepare your home to sell.

❑ Begin an education process and present all available alternatives.

❑ Prepare a market analysis to establish fair market value.

❑ Prepare and explain the listing contract, often a six-month signed agreement.

❑ Transmit listing details to the Multiple Listing Service (MLS) and Internet for immediate distribution.

❑ Place for-sale signs on property and design advertising media.

❑ Notify top local agents of the new listing.

❑ Schedule property for a broker's open house/agent tour.

❑ Create facts and features sheets and distribute according to plans.

❑ Immediately call all current buyers who may be interested.

❑ Arrange showings for other agents and plan open house dates.

❑ Create contact calender dates for verbal progress reports.

❑ Review marketing activities with you and adjust as necessary.

❑ Screen and prequalify all potential buyers.

❑ Present and discuss all offers on property with owner(s).

❑ Negotiate the transaction with other agents.

❑ Finalize the sales contract and arrange inspections, appraisals, repairs, and closing day.

❑ Accompany sellers at the closing and follow up to ensure any remaining seller needs are met.

It's delicate work, and many agents don't risk offending you for fear of losing a sale. In my work, I have always asked a prospective seller, "Are you sure you want to sell it?" I'll ask questions to understand why they want to or must sell.

The reason I do that is because you don't always have to sell the goose (house) to get the golden egg (money). You can rent it out and use equity lines to get all of that money, and still keep the asset with no money being thrown away to sell it. Also, it is a tax shelter, so you could be throwing that away, too.

Let me explain something: Most people think that to buy another house, they must sell their existing one. No, no, no! The bank thinks like this: Say you have a $100,000 house and your mortgage is $700 a month. As long as you have a signed one-year (or longer) lease agreement, which in essence says the tenants will be paying the mortgage, the bank is fine with that. What they do is factor 75 percent of that rent payment as a mortgage obligation offset. Assume you get $1,000 a month for rent (1 percent of your house's value is usually a good gauge for monthly rent rate). So 75 percent of $1,000 is $750. You actually are able to qualify for more on your next house because the rent payment exceeds your mortgage payment! The old house is paying for itself plus generating additional money.

So that is why, in some cases, I will discourage my clients from selling. A full-time agent rarely does that. It's not their fault. They just don't have the time to educate you and explain how to be a landlord too. This book is meant to teach you that!

I create advantages for my clients' long-term financial health. I want to give them every opportunity to be able to make the best choice for themselves based on all the possible alternatives that they potentially have at their disposal. This process takes time. Trust is not built overnight, so that gives you an idea why in some cases, it just is not attempted.

The point? There is a point. If a real estate agent has given you this book, odds are extremely good that you have found an agent who truly cares more about your needs than their own. They are not afraid to educate you. They are not afraid to lose a sale. They are not there to take a one-time shot with you. They are long-term relationship builders and these people are rare— believe it!

There are other factors, such as conflicting personality styles, character traits, mannerisms, temperament, and so forth. So in the end you're going to want a capable professional who cares more about your needs than their own, and who you also get along with! If they don't return your calls or you feel as though they are too busy to answer your questions and/or educate you properly, then look for another agent.

If you have received this book from a real estate professional, I would certainly invite him or her over for a little discussion about your real estate needs. After all, they know the potential of this book and they have had the guts to give it to you despite that fact! These are smart agents. They actually make their job easier by educating you through a book. This helps them by having you understand what needs to be done to succeed in your real estate goals.

If you do find this rare agent of whom I speak, and you choose to use this person or not, ask for his or her business card. Refer this person to everyone you know who is going to require a real estate broker or agent's services. You will be doing everyone a favor by giving them good advice and that, my friend, is what this book is all about. Help other people. Please don't forget—that is my personal Magic Bullet. It is the most powerful of them all.

● Advantages of Having a Buyer's Agent on Your Team

As a well-rounded real estate investor, I recommend you have a loyal buyer's agent on your team of network partners. Throughout the book I effectively show you how to sell property on your own. At this point I would like to show you why having the advantage of a loyal buyer's agent when purchasing property is a very wise move.

A buyer's agent protects your interests in real estate. By signing a client representation agreement with you and disclosing this buyer's agency relationship status to the sellers through their listing agent, the buyer's agent has effectively complied with all real estate regulations allowing them to now work for you and *your* best interests.

Once accepted, this agent can begin to disclose pertinent facts, which they as seller's agents or subagents of the seller's agent could not ordinarily disclose. What once would have been a breach of contract is now eliminated in your favor and you can begin using the power of a full-fledged and knowledgeable agent to *your* best advantage.

Your client privilege with this agent allows them first to protect your identity and keep all details confidential, which protects your position. They can guide, investigate, disclose, suggest, plan, orchestrate, prepare, and deliver multiple offers using their strategy, expertise, negotiating and bargaining skills in your favor with the seller often paying their commission through the listing agent's commission split!

Wow, harnessing the power of the pro for free! If the selling agent doesn't agree to split the commission then you have a choice of paying your buyer's agent yourself, or moving on to another seller whose agent *is* willing to split the fee to satisfy their seller's need to get the property sold.

A good buyer's agent will be familiar with all properties that are listed for sale in your area and often knows of property that no one else does. Frequently agents know of sellers who haven't listed property but with an offer in hand would be willing to sell. These agents draw from experience, contacts, relationships, and insider knowledge that ordinary citizens just don't have.

By using them you'll know when a good buy comes up. Whether the sellers are nearing foreclosure, bankruptcy, death, divorce, relocation, or any numbers of reasons for an immediate sale, this agent can tell you why. They can also bring to your attention reasons why not to buy, such as poor design, construction, location, better buys elsewhere, and so forth, For all the reasons stated, I highly recommend including this most superior bird dog in your overall plans for succeeding in the fields of investment opportunity.

As an investor you may find that a good agent who understands your objectives, knows the market, and has properties of their own can be a valuable asset in your investment plan. The agent should have access to the MLS and will know of many potential properties to alert you to a good deal. Just remain loyal to them when they inform you of a deal and close it through them. The sellers are paying the commission, so if it's a really good deal then why not let that bird dog hunt for you, in essence, for free.

Loyalty, fidelity, devotion, and trust
are the keys to making it work!

● ● ● ● CAPTURED IDEAS ● ● ● ●

Notes—*insights, ideas, actions to take*

_____

_____

_____

_____

_____

_____

Strategy—*planning for success*

_____

_____

_____

_____

_____

_____

Tactics—*ways to achieve success*

_____

_____

_____

_____

_____

_____

Chapter 5

Networking Basics

These Magic Bullets involve personality, ability, motivation, resources, experience, organizational skills, risk acceptance, a mission/plan with an end in mind, and courage to do the following things as best you can.

Relax. You've got what it takes.

If it's real estate you want, go get it. Start attending local conferences, meetings, and seminars. Begin by surrounding yourself with high-energy believers. Be a bee. If you want honey, find a hive with activity and contribute your share. The nectar you deliver is found in planes, trains, automobiles, hotels, motels, shops, and stores. You network at every opportunity and it never stops.

Use filters to decide which people work for you. Ask yourself the following. Does the person offer advice, referrals, information, support, or energy? Can the person mentor or introduce you to someone who is willing to spend the time necessary to shift your paradigm? Will this person accelerate your learning and provide greater understanding on your subject of interest? Can you reciprocate and return value to the person in some way?

You gain power by taking risks and stepping out of your comfort zone. Risk taking in real estate might be committing to buy a property that presents challenges, talking to owners who are difficult, or suggesting alternative solutions to seemingly unresolvable situations.

You may risk time and money on classes, books, and tests. You may risk looking the fool with a stupid question. You may risk losing a deal by presenting a low offer. The point is you learn a tremendous amount about what you took the risk on and you get better with every attempt.

Let's say you have done and continue to practice what we have discussed so far. Based on that, you now will have something to offer. How can you specifically offer assistance to others and expand your network?

Once again, you reach out and add value to others by giving them the power you have gained. Through your trial, error, and success, you now can influence favorable outcomes in the lives of others by saving them time and money, and by showing them easier, more efficient, effective ways to succeed. By being enthusiastic through your confident, supporting attitude, you give them more power, energy, confidence, performance, profit potential, and focus.

Who in real estate can further educate me or support me in my quest for more information? How about attorneys, bankers, mortgage brokers, home inspectors, appraisers, title company officers, surveyors, insurance agents, real estate agents, current landlords, rental managers, and CPAs?

What about basic education from plumbers, electricians, heating/air-conditioning techs, roofers, carpenters, flooring specialists, painters, landscapers, and appliance repairmen? What do these people represent? How can you learn from them? Primarily you go for their expertise. Ask them to tell you what it is exactly they do and how they do it. Be interested in the mechanics of their profession.

Use your imagination and engage your allies. Grow your network. One person at a time. Whenever someone is willing to give you a piece of him- or herself, take it. Draw out the best they have to give. If you want an education in perfecting these techniques, go buy the paperback version of Dale Carnegie's

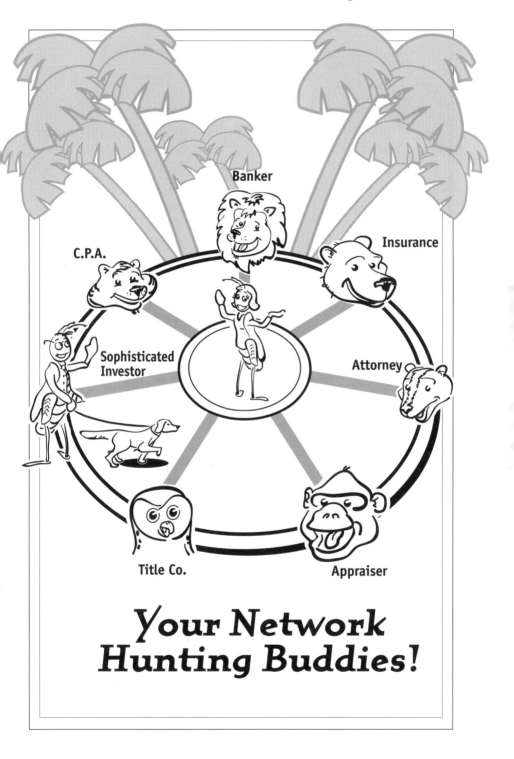

Your Network
Hunting Buddies!

classic, *How to Win Friends and Influence People.* The essence of the book is to listen and be sincerely interested in the other person. Praise and appreciate them. You may also offer them exciting challenges to further your relations.

In order to develop your personality, you must get over the fear of rejection. That fear will hold you back! Get over it. Forget about it and move on. You'll grow as a result.

Practicing the techniques used to conquer fear of rejection will lead you to gain more and more ability in dealing with and understanding people. If you will forget about *you* and sincerely and compassionately listen to other people when they talk to you, they often will mesmerize you with what they say. Now step into their shoes and try to solve, understand, feel, or relate to what is being said.

Take the focus off of you, and your fears won't be a problem. When you get out of yourself, it's impossible to be self-conscious. Use empathy as a tool to motivate you to further action. When you understand and feel how someone else feels, from their point of view, you can move to the next step, which is commitment.

Now you offer your ability and resources to give them what they need. Odds are you have experienced something in your past that you can offer as a possible new avenue of approach. Help them organize a plan of attack. You strategize and help them implement the tactics necessary to achieve their objective or solve a problem. Call upon your network to help you accomplish their goal.

When you save people like this, you put another knot in your safety net, and by helping someone else you gain more power. Your network gets larger, and your options and alternatives grow. You can safely accept risk when you're helping others because you personally have nothing to lose and everything to gain.

● ● ● ● CAPTURED IDEAS ● ● ● ●

Notes—*insights, ideas, actions to take*

_____

_____

_____

_____

_____

Strategy—*planning for success*

_____

_____

_____

_____

_____

Tactics—*ways to achieve success*

_____

_____

_____

_____

_____

Chapter 6

Protecting Yourself

    I believe in educating oneself in real estate, but you won't find me recommending you obtain a real estate license. A real estate license can actually hold you back from being a savvy investor. First, you have to announce to every seller that you are an agent. It's an ethics rule and a disclosure law. Once you do that, the seller is on guard for all kinds of reasons and you waste precious time overcoming negative reactions.

    Second, when you go to sell your real estate, the same things apply but add to that scenario the fact that if you make large profits on property that you sell, people can come after you, saying you took advantage of them because of your expertise. To protect yourself in these cases, you must by law disclose the fact that you are *a licensed agent and that you intend to make a profit from the transaction.* You don't have the advantage of playing the unsophisticated buyer or seller role as a strict unlicensed investor would. You should also write a statement to that effect at the bottom of your contract and have the other party sign it, in this way protecting yourself from litigation later.

    So you don't need to go to college for four years and you don't need a real estate license. Go out and do it, using a lawyer to protect you every step of the way. Simply weave into every agreement or offer you make the following statement: *This entire agreement is subject to my attorney's approval.* I can't

emphasize enough the importance of this one line of text. It covers everything. It gives you time to investigate deals. It protects your interests and keeps you from getting burned in this business.

Here are a couple more beauties I use to protect myself, and you should too. These are used with initial purchase offers:

- *Willing to pay X amount of dollars or appraised value, whichever is less.* What this means is that you are only going to pay so much, but if the appraisal is lower than what you offered, you get the property for the lower price.

- *Subject to my partner's approval.* My partner was always my wife, and if she didn't like it, the deal was null and void, cancelled, over, kaput, finito.

Those are examples of escape clauses that could be abused to the point of being called "weasel clauses." Don't be a *weasel!* They give you a short period of time to have the option to buy something first with the right to cancel the deal, contingent upon something or someone else's decision. I use them to protect myself and to get a little time to do my research on the property. Don't use them to unfairly tie a seller's hands. Be fair and try to move quickly when you do use them.

Here is a little trick I use occasionally to protect myself. I don't use it very often but it can be used in a fair manner. When you write an offer to purchase property, on the top line of the contract is a line that indicates who the buyer is. On that line in certain cases, I will write my name plus the words "or assigns." What the word "assigns" does is this: It allows me to sell by assigning my right to buy the property to someone else. Dirty dealers will take advantage of people with that word if they can get away with it.

When you assign something to someone else, you are transferring your right, or contract, to another person—often for a fee. For example, say you have a home under contract with the seller for $150,000. You have added the words "or assigns" behind your name on the buyer's line. If the seller accepts this contract, you in turn could sell the home or your right to buy the home for a higher price if you found someone willing to pay that higher price.

It can be useful in situations where the property is distressed—the fixer-uppers, the abandoned, the condemned. I go a step further and look for distressed sellers, such as those selling because of death, divorce, or relocation. Frequently, however, the available property is not the type I specialize in. But if it's a real steal, and I can get it for 40 or 50 percent off its true fair market value, I will assign it to someone who does deal in that type of property and make a profit by assigning it.

For example, say I pay $90,000 for a distressed cosmetic rehab since I bought it at 40 percent off fair market value, or $36,000 under market. I may choose to sell or assign my right to buy it for $10,000 and let the new buyer fix it, live in it, rent it, sell it, or whatever.

I always let the seller know what I am doing. If it is a problem for the seller, I will buy it outright, then flip it. But it costs more to do this, so I'll explain this to the seller and get their permission to use it. Again, do not try to slip it by the seller; always tell them what you are doing. You will have a miserable existence if you practice real estate by deceit. Purpose, passion, and desire cannot be achieved or acquired by deceit.

Soon you are going to be face-to-face and toe-to-toe with a real live seller. Now is the time to ask more questions, take notes, and do preliminary fact-finding and a general inspection of the property. Odds are good at this point that your fears are going to get the best of you. You may not be confident enough yet to make an offer, even if you put in the escape clauses to protect yourself. Let me stop here and give you one bulletproof escape clause: *This offer is subject to my partner's approval.* Since your partner isn't there, the seller will agree to this and give you time to get that partner to further investigate. This so-called partner of yours can be anyone. Mine was my wife. If she didn't like it, the deal was canceled. But who says your partner can't be your dog! If there is no fire hydrant, your partner just canceled the contingent agreement.

Now you have time to go and get your sophisticated investor friend to help you judge this property's potential. After you've gone through a few of these types of situations, you will get a general feeling of confidence back. You will acclimate yourself to the process of evaluating potential deals and making preliminary offers to lock in your position or option to buy it first within a certain period of time.

This is why you need that sophisticated investor friend. He or she will act as a neutral third party in getting the details of your contract ironed out. This person can protect you and defuse the direct confrontation between buyers and sellers. This is just one of the reasons why real estate agents are here to stay, because they are the grease that helps to keep the deal from getting too fouled up to the point the deal falls through.

Any ideas yet? Put them down under "Captured Ideas" below!

● ● ● ● CAPTURED IDEAS ● ● ● ●

Notes—*insights, ideas, actions to take*

_____

_____

_____

_____

_____

_____

Strategy—*planning for success*

_____

_____

_____

_____

_____

Tactics—*ways to achieve success*

_____

_____

_____

_____

_____

_____

Chapter 7

Marketing, Finding, and Closing the Deals

When you're ready to make your first deal, I suggest you start calling "for sale by owners" out of the classified section of the newspaper. Ask them all the questions you can up to the point they have had enough (see below for a list of questions) or you find the property is not of interest to you. If you are interested, schedule to meet them at the property so you can view it in person. (If they are difficult to talk to on the phone, they may be difficult in person, so brace yourself!)

If you can't immediately get through to the for-sale-by-owner properties, go to www.AnyWho.com. If you have a phone number, this website will give you the address. Use your street finder to go straight to the property and see it immediately. Beat less educated hunters.

Place this basic ad in your local paper's real estate section to appear on Sunday. If you can afford to run the ad seven days a week, do it. You won't miss any sellers who need to act fast. Negotiate with the newspaper for a better rate.

> I buy properties. Will pay a fair price w/small down pmt. Quick closings. Call (your name) at (your number).

Following is a list of questions—a script, of sorts—you can use when talking to sellers:

Do you own the property?

If the answer is yes, you can continue with the next question. But if the answer is no, then you'll want to find out who the owner is.

The following are possible answers to that question with some likely scenarios:

● The owner is someone who lives out of town and is unfamiliar with current market conditions.

● The owner is incompetent to negotiate and someone else, with a power of attorney, is acting on his or her behalf.

● The owner passed away and the executor of his or her estate is acting on his or her behalf. This could translate into a quick, easy sale.

● A real estate broker or organized selling entity is the owner. The property may be overpriced.

● A bank officer or foreclosure agency is selling the property. This is an indication you may want to lower your offer.

● The property is being sold via a sophisticated lease optioning reseller or investor. Be careful not to let a shrewd seller outwit you or get the better end of the deal.

Why are you selling?

The more you know the motivation behind the sale, the better you can solve the problem. Here are some of the most common reasons:

● The owners are getting a divorce. Often two parties must agree, signaling a distress sale, "don't wanters," bad memories.

● One of the owners has died. This can often mean a quick sale, but emotions may be running high, so be considerate and tactful.

● The owners are relocating. This frequently means the seller is looking for a quick sale and closing.

● The owners are downsizing. This is usually done by "empty nesters," whose children have moved away. Ask if they would be willing to carry the financing.

● The owners are moving to a larger home. These sellers will probably wait to get their price, which may be high.

● There is a foreclosure looming. These owners will probably be willing to negotiate. You may also inquire about making up delinquent payments and taking over their mortgage, i.e., short sale.

● The owners have a new home already and need to sell quickly.

● The property was a rental, and the owner is tired of it and wants to cash out. This is probably a sophisticated seller, but may be a serious "don't wanter." (Ask if they have any more rentals for sale!)

How long have you owned the property? How old is it?

● If the owner has had it for a long time, equity could be quite large. Ask about owner financing.

● If the property has been owned a short time, there is little or no equity. Inquire further as to whether this is a reseller—an investor who is turning the property around quickly to sell for a profit—or a fixer-upper. Divorce, transfer, or a lost job could also be possibilities.

● If the property was built after 1978, no lead-based paint disclosure is required. (We'll discuss lead paint later.)

● If the property was built before 1988, financing may be fully assumable. Ask!

● If the property is 30 years or older, a professional inspection is a must. Check electrical, plumbing, and heating systems closely. (Even new homes should be inspected carefully.)

● If the property is 50 years or older, it might be difficult to finance.

● Ask how many previous owners there have been and why the current owner bought it.

Have there been or are there any existing problems with the property that you know of?

● "Well, yes, it has (fill in the blank)." You must decide if you want to deal with it.

● "I don't know," "I'm not sure," or "I don't think so." Get a signed disclosure statement and a home inspection. The owner may be concealing defects.

Can you tell me a little about the property?

This is the catchall question. When you ask this question, be quiet and let them fill the voids of silence. Ask open-ended questions that get them talking. You want their rambling life story. With this question, you may get the whole story, the true facts behind the sale. It's one more chance to get them to volunteer information. Probe! Ask what, why, where, when, how, who? Anything else I should know?

When can I see it?

Schedule a showing for daylight hours and don't go alone. Bring a knowledgeable assistant for evaluation purposes and safety. Try to see it as soon as possible. If it's a good deal, it might be sold before you ever get there. Schedule as many as you can and see more than one while you're out, if possible. Don't forget your street finder, newspaper, notes, phone, flashlight, and offer sheets (available from your attorney or websites such as www.audrie.com; www.USLegalForms.com; www.kaktus.com, or www.UrgentBusiness.com—many for free).

These questions begin to either interlock with previous questions or contradict them. Use them to cross-check previous questions and answers, develop your gut feeling, get clarity, and root out deception! (Use all your scripts with this in mind.)

If a seller has scheduled several interested buyers to see the property at the same time, don't act irrationally because of perceived competition. In other words, don't get sucked into an auction atmosphere.

Note: If *you* are selling, have your answers ready and be prepared to answer the same questions.

Back to hunting! Where can you find properties?

● Look at bulletin boards, local papers, and small independent publications. This goes for every publication you get. Make sure you get one of the first copies off the press. Go to the facility that houses the presses and get your copy before the ink has a chance to dry. Let no one beat you to the punch.

● Better yet, advertise yourself and get people who are thinking about selling to call you before they actually tell the world through an ad.

● Look at the legal section of the newspapers. Contact heirs, attorneys, and sales in the garage or estate sale sections. Also, 20 percent of people who have garage sales are planning on moving soon. Ask about the house or their neighbors' homes. Always keep your antenna up! Your odds of success increase when you choose large population centers and remain in the market constantly on the lookout for your type of deal.

● Look for vacant houses that are run down, fire damaged, abandoned, or with city notices evident. Talk to the neighbors of these homes. They usually know who owns it and what is going on. They have an interest in seeing it restored to beauty. You can also find the owner through public records databases. In many counties, these records are available online. It's too bad you can't look in the mailbox to see who is receiving mail at the property in question, but that would be too easy.

● Don't be afraid to walk up to a property and look in a window to confirm that it is indeed vacant. But be careful; don't endanger yourself by getting bit by a dog—or worse. Use common sense. Contact out-of-state owners through property records, by letter, and/or phone. Leave your business card on the door!

Make friends with your local lenders and let them know you are the one to call when they have a foreclosure looming or in progress. Hint: If you will get preapproved with lenders beforehand, they may call upon you sooner. Lenders will also have properties that went into foreclosure, then to auction. If the home doesn't sell at auction, it goes back to the lender as OREO, or *other real estate owned*. These kinds of properties might be just what you are looking for.

Again, watch the local paper for foreclosure auctions, tax sales, HUD, and VA listed properties. Note: Auctions held in bad weather where the property absolutely must be sold are your best chance to limit competition and get property at rock-bottom prices. Because there is no low limit on what can be accepted (that is, no reserve), you might win big.

If you find yourself dealing with a real estate agent, remember that it is their job to sell you something. When you approach them, be very specific about what you want and tell them to call only if they have something that satisfies your investment guidelines.

Ask agents to give you those expired listings they couldn't sell. Suggest a 2 percent commission if they will assist with the paperwork after you make the deal with the seller on your own.

Don't be selective. If the property *is* an absolute steal, buy it, then turn around and sell it immediately to somebody who likes to work with that type of real estate. This is not necessarily limited to distressed properties, but rather any type of property that can be had at a price that is significantly below market, then resold at a profit. For example, you may not deal in mobile homes, but if you can get a $30,000 mobile home for $10,000, you could quickly sell it for $15,000 to an investor of that type of housing. This is true for condos and residential lots as well. Get the option and hand it off to another buyer. Look for distressed sellers in addition to distressed property.

Make up flyers to get the word out about what you do. For instance, "I pay $500 to you at closing if I buy a house you told me about! Do you know anyone who is selling property? Please call (your name) at (your number)." Post flyers everywhere—colleges, laundromats, shopping centers, bowling alleys, public bulletin boards, churches, and local businesses. Wherever large numbers of people congregate, give them a chance to give you a lead on a hot deal. In your everyday business dealings with property managers, moving companies, relocation services, neighbors, landlords, tenants, the mailman, the paper boy, gardeners, landscapers, service technicians, pest control people, friends, acquaintances, relatives, and other investors, make sure they know they can make $500 if you buy a property they tell you about.

Get some quality business cards printed up—I recommend 10,000—and hand them out to everyone you know. Give each of your soldiers stacks of your cards for exponential growth. Be sure your offer of the $500 bounty is printed on the cards. (A special note here: Water, gas, and electric company personnel who shut off utility meters can be very good bird dogs, when it comes to finding property that is in trouble or vacant. Make sure these people have your business card.)

Here are some additional ideas for finding those deals:

- Put up signs telling people you buy real estate. Telephone poles, roadsides, high traffic corners.

- Join organizations. There are so many—pick those that truly interest you and let it be known you pay bounties for consummated (closed) deals.

- When you use headhunters—your personal bounty hunters—leave out no one.

- As your business grows, you might consider television, radio, phone books, billboards, street benches, bumper stickers, and bigger commissions paid to those who help you find the deals. Use your imagination.

- Make multiple lowball offers on overpriced properties and walk away. Don't deposit earnest money but they may stew on your offer and call you a month later, accepting your deal. Leave the offer with them.

● Older people can be valuable informants—especially those who live in older neighborhoods. They frequently know everything about the neighborhood.

● Attend free seminars on real estate. Not only will you learn about real estate, but you can also capture names and circulate among real estate–minded people. Once you have their names, call your own club meeting and network to prosperity. Find your mentor here.

● Go to where people are buying for-sale-by-owner signs. Ask them what they are selling. Follow them home and get the first look. Be first or lose the deal!

● Try offering 15 percent less than what you are willing to pay. You never know—the seller may accept it. If he or she doesn't, you can still negotiate up to 15 percent more and get it for what you originally were willing to pay. Any higher, walk away but leave the offer on the table (the offer stands).

● Make your offer easy for the seller to understand. Get the option to buy, but use a contingency to protect yourself. Iron out the details later but lock it up now!

● Buy properties from sellers who tend not to care: corporations, disinterested heirs, nonprofits, and probate attorneys. Also check out seized or foreclosed properties and those being sold in a tax sale and at private auctions.

● Assist someone in selling his or her property even if you don't want it. Be a friend and offer to help for nothing in return. You will be amazed at what happens when you do this with no thought of making money. This is a Magic Bullet in disguise.

Those are some of the basics of advertising and finding the opportunities to buy real estate below market price. As the old saying goes, *you make your profit when you buy, not when you sell.*

There is no doubt in my mind that if you use your creative imagination to explore other potential ways to find bargain opportunities, you will in fact come up with some excellent ideas concerning your local area and the properties that are available

(e.g., pizza drivers, police officers, bail bondsmen). Think bird dog!

Above all, don't get discouraged! There are investors out there who will look at close to a hundred properties and narrow their decision down to two or three candidates, finally choosing only one. Sometimes the deal will appear at number 27 or it may come at 85; you never know when or at what point fate will give in and surrender to your relentless pursuit of the deal.

Eventually, as a result of your great hunting prowess, you are going to have a deal to transact. First-time buyers or people who haven't practiced buying or selling in a while tend to get rusty or be unfamiliar with this series of events.

Get the option to buy contingent on something—the inspection report, the appraisal, financing, and so forth. Use an attorney, sophisticated mentor, or agent to review your preliminary paperwork and when you're convinced that you have the finer details and facts of the deal properly defined, investigated, verified, and attested to, or otherwise agreed upon, remove the contingencies and fully execute the deal. Hint: Again remember to write on your option-to-buy contract that you are willing to pay whatever you have agreed upon or appraised value, whichever is less. Don't pay over appraised value.

Once the contract is signed and agreed to by both you and the seller, your earnest money check will be made out and given to the title company you are working with and where the closing will likely take place. The title company holds the earnest money in trust, as a neutral third party. They will apply this check to the purchase price during the closing process, thus reducing the amounts you owe by the amount of your earnest money deposit.

If that sounds complicated, don't worry. It's not that difficult. Here is what you do:

- ● Make copies of everything.
- ● Give copies to yourself, the sellers, your chosen title company, and your lender, plus anyone else who may be involved—attorney, mentor, agent, and so forth.

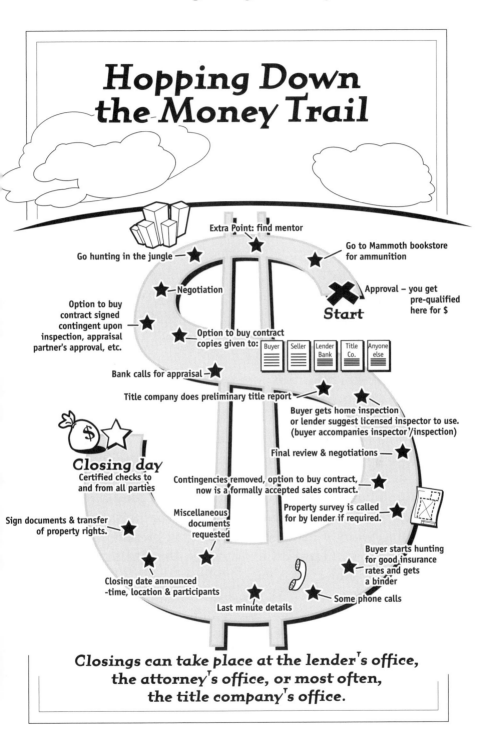

Hopping Down the Money Trail

Extra Point: find mentor

Go hunting in the jungle — ★

Go to Mammoth bookstore for ammunition

★ Negotiation

Approval – you get pre-qualified here for $

Option to buy contract signed contingent upon inspection, appraisal partner's approval, etc.

Start

Option to buy contract copies given to: Buyer | Seller | Lender Bank | Title Co. | Anyone else

Bank calls for appraisal — ★

Title company does preliminary title report ★ ★

Buyer gets home inspection or lender suggest licensed inspector to use. (buyer accompanies inspector / inspection)

Final review & negotiations — ★

Closing day
Certified checks to and from all parties

Contingencies removed, option to buy contract, now is a formally accepted sales contract.

Miscellaneous documents requested

Property survey is called for by lender if required.

Sign documents & transfer of property rights. — ★

Buyer starts hunting for good insurance rates and gets a binder

Closing date announced -time, location & participants

Last minute details

Some phone calls

Closings can take place at the lender's office, the attorney's office, or most often, the title company's office.

● Give everyone involved roughly 45 days from the day you sign your contract to complete the processing of the deal. Some closings are sooner, some later…it varies.

● Take your cues from the title company, your lender, your attorney, or agent. They have a duty and responsibility to protect your interests as well as their own. The lender is going to ensure the collateral (property) has value equal to or more than the amount being borrowed and the title company is going to ensure the title is clear for sale.

● Keep in contact with all the players—sellers, bank, title company, attorney, and so forth—and keep the ball rolling, right up to the closing table. There are specific deadlines set for things like the appraisal, the title search, the financing; make sure those deadlines are met. On closing day, you'll sign the transfer documentation and conclude the deal.

● Taxes and Records

Okay, so you've made your first deal and you're feeling pretty good about yourself. But wait. Did you save every receipt, every bill, every closing document? Before you move on to your next great deal, get yourself a big folder or file, and label that thing with this property's address. You are going to want to save every single scrap of paper that has to do with that property.

You simply must use a CPA at tax time. A good one will save you his or her fee plus a lot more when you let them perform their magic. I have had the same CPA tax preparer for the last 14 years and I will profess to the world that Matthew is worth his weight in gold. He has saved his fee in the first 15 minutes of our meeting every year. Matt is a Magic Bullet I use to face the IRS man every year. Your CPA should guide and protect you.

Don't cheat on your taxes. This will knock you out. A good CPA will keep you honest *and* save you money! Don't misunderstand me. I am telling you to take every legal deduction you are entitled to—and there are many. In order to do this, you must keep every receipt and expense record to prove your case.

First Year Deductions

Concerning rental property here are the major first year tax deductions allowed as a result of your purchase. (Your closing statement will have most of these listed.)

- The costs of title, fire, and liability insurance
- Amount of property tax paid by you in that year
- All interest of the loans on the property
- Various escrow and lender fees

Annual Deductions

These may include but are not limited by the following:

- Mortgage/loans interest, taxes, insurance
- All utilities paid by you
- All repairs made to the property, landscaping and cleaning included
- Advertising and management fees
- City licenses, fees, and taxes
- Vehicle maintenance and mileage, tools, office expenses, etc.
- If your rental property is out of state, your air fare, lodging, rental car, and meals are now going to be used to offset your taxes as well, when attending to your rental property matters—icing on the cake!

Long Life Depreciated

These items are often categorized as capital expenses and as such need to be depreciated over the period of the item's useful life.

- New mechanicals, plumbing, electrical, central heat/air, dishwashers, etc.
- Additions, roofing, fencing, siding, gutters, landscaping, resurfacing, etc.
- Carpets, windows, kitchen remodels, window treatments, etc.

You keep the records and receipts, and your accountant will do the rest!

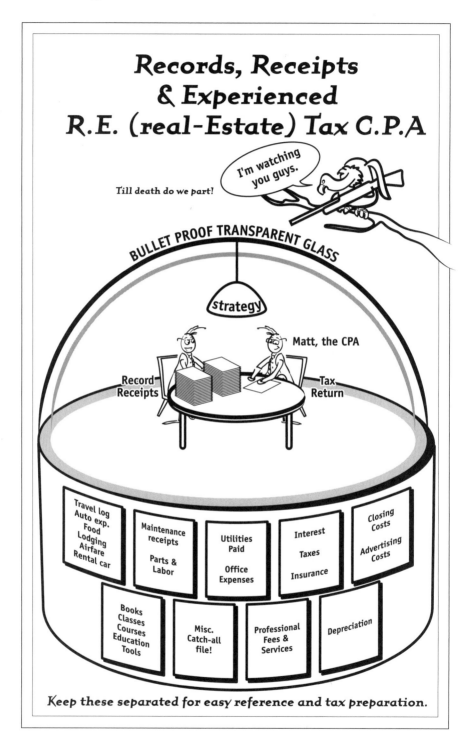

● Total Operating Expenses

Here is one more way to look at expenses. Save those receipts!

Fixed Expenses

● Taxes

● Insurance

● License fees, etc.

These stay relatively the same every year with slight increases usually being the case. You pay for these whether occupied or vacant.

Variable Expenses

● Management fees

● Advertising and leasing fees

● Utilities, i.e., water, sewer, garbage, electricity, gas, etc.

● Heat/air-conditioning

● Cleaning, decorating

● General maintenance and repair of structure

● Grounds and parking maintenance

● Miscellaneous, e.g., supplies, dump fees, pest control, security measures

By limiting the number of occupants and services provided, you'll generally lower variable expenses.

Replacement Reserves

● Roof coverings

● Carpeting, vinyl, tile, and wood floor coverings

● Kitchen, bath, and laundry equipment

● Water heaters, major components of air-conditioning equipment, etc.

● Structural items of limited life such as fences, sheds, etc.

● Sidewalks, driveways, and parking areas

● Exterior painting, patching, and repair

You would be wise to set aside enough each month to periodically replace items that wear out more rapidly than the building itself. If the previous owner has deferred these maintenance items, lower your offer accordingly to prepare for their replacement sooner.

● ● ● ● CAPTURED IDEAS ● ● ● ●

Notes—*insights, ideas, actions to take*

_____

_____

_____

_____

Strategy—*planning for success*

_____

_____

_____

_____

Tactics—*ways to achieve success*

_____

_____

_____

_____

Chapter 8

A Finance Primer— From Borrowing to Using Equity

Yes, folks, that's right. In the continuing saga of *Magic Bullets of Real Estate* wisdom, you're going to get a right-brain thinker's views on using the avenues of approach to financing all the deals you can envision.

Before we get started, I want to ask you a question. Who loans money? The Federal Reserve, commercial banks, insurance companies, mortgage backed securities, lenders such as Fannie Mae, Freddie Mac/HUD, local savings and loans, credit unions, mortgage brokers, wealthy private individuals, the sellers themselves, and credit agencies of various organized structures including companies that market credit card products.

How about a wealthy family member, partner, or friend? Maybe equity lines, or yourself, in the form of personal savings? Or what about using brainpower to creatively structure deals using no money at all?

If you're counting on me to tell you one surefire, easy method, then keep reading. The only infallible advice I can offer is to bombard you with ideas and let you come to your own Magic Bullet solution. We all have very different situations, and as a result, your options will be different from mine.

Here's your first Magic Bullet: Institutions don't lend money, people do! A building can't approve or disapprove anything so you're going to have to understand people and how they think in order to persuade them into seeing how you can help them by getting the loan. You fill their quotas.

The people who decide whether or not you're getting financing have to know in their own mind that you're not going to jeopardize their own financial security. They don't want to be fired or go broke or have to fight you in court, or anything else that requires time, effort, and money just to break even. These people want a benefit, not a headache.

The first thing you can do to build trust in the mind of your benefactor, or lender, is to show them you have done your homework. What this means is you must have as many of the details as you can gather concerning the reason you need the money. People are reasoning creatures. If you don't make sense, your odds of success are marginal at best. So the number one way to get money is to create trust in the minds of those who control the purse strings.

You create trust through credit scores, tax returns, work history, and net worth assets and liabilities worksheets. Every lender wants those things up front, so gather them together and make copies to give to him or her upon your first meeting.

Bring the following items to your meeting:

● W-2s

● Tax returns for the past two years

● Three months of bank statements

● A copy of your credit report (although the lender will also likely run its own)

● A filled-out loan application

● Copies of titles to good collateral (if any)

● Three references

● The name of the person willing to co-sign, if possible

The best time to ask for a loan is when you don't need it. Now does that make sense? Yes, it does! Here's why: You need to build trust and you should take a little time beforehand to do that.

Think about who you personally could use to get a loan and then provide them with copies of your aforementioned self-worth documents. Let them research your documentation, and you will be entitled to their time in further discussing your wants, needs, and desires. Once you build relationships, a phone call is all it takes to get whatever you want if it coincides or makes sense with what you have already discussed and planned for.

I started out 14 years ago by getting small loans of $60,000 to $70,000, and those were the hardest to get because the lenders had to verify and trust what I said, backed by my history, which was represented by pieces of paper. If you want to accelerate the trust-building phase of your financial relationship, provide collateral and high-level references. That way you have something to lose and your high level references give you their permission to use their reputations and good name to validate you. You might consider getting a cosigner for added security and higher loan amounts.

Organization and planning will help you prepare for your loan. As I have mentioned previously, I also encourage you to go to a free homebuyer's education class. These are usually held free in your community and will give you a basic introduction to real estate finance. I go all the time to refresh my memory. Plus, it avails me of current loan products, rates, and programs that can be used to my advantage.

What types of loan products are available? There are veteran loan (VA) guarantees, first-time buyer loans, HUD 203 rehabilitation loans, FHA, conventional bank loans, fixed rate loans, variable rates, graduated payment loans, low income loans, personal loans—and hundreds more.

What category do you fit into? That's for you to figure out with some free help, of course. Go to the homebuyer class and talk to some lenders. And don't forget mortgage brokers! Mortgage brokers are a special type of animal. These wily beasts more often than not have more access to money than most anyone you will meet. It is because they are brokers—in essence, middlemen. They find lenders and borrowers and create a marriage. They often know of many routes to take to obtain financing for your situation.

They deal with banks; money markets; insurance companies; wealthy, private investors; and they themselves have money to lend on occasion. The bottom line is they can often get you a loan that the people they represent wouldn't give you personally. These brokers will package a bunch of loans together and sell them as one large financial interest-bearing product that has been scrutinized, verified, and prepared in accordance with the preapproved buyer's guidelines.

Insurance companies, pension funds, bond funds, and financial stock purchasers will invest in you through this larger secured product. Your loan has been sold at that point to someone else as a long-term investment.

Now picture this: Here is the right-brain thinker's view of things. The right-brain lives in space, seeing things in pictures and grandiosity. They always have an idea and a million questions to go with it. They ask, "Why can't, what if, how about, why not, how come?" and to top it off, they will attempt to ring out the left-brain analytical types like a sponge, to collect further information to achieve their objective. These people include artists, salespeople, public speakers, entertainers, designers, and politicians.

Well, when the smoke clears and the left-brain numbers-cruncher gets over the initial shock of being blasted by the onslaught of right-brained gibberish, there's usually a period of silence. So you know what happens? Yep, the right-brain extrovert starts talking again. At this point, the financial person is being asked to find some financial solution to the problem.

Normally, they can't do it and stubbornly refuse to even consider alternatives because of the approach used by the right-brainer. What often happens is you will get a request for more information, documentation, and research. They're looking for numbers because they use qualifying ratios to solve problems. Here's what I mean.

If you're talking about a standard home loan, a 28/36 ratio is often used. What that says is 28 percent of your monthly income can be used to pay the mortgage principal, mortgage interest, property taxes, and property insurance. If you make $3,000 a month, you can afford to spend $840 a month on housing. That's the front ratio.

The back ratio is 36 percent. The lender says that up to 36 percent of your total monthly income can go toward paying for the mortgage plus credit card loans, auto/boat loans, student loans, and so forth.

Well, that leaves 64 percent left over. Why don't they count some of that? Here's why. You often need that much a month to pay for electricity, phone, cable, water, sewer, garbage, heat, clothes, food, car insurance, gas and repairs, entertainment, furniture, toys, doodads, knickknacks, and everything else you come across that sounds like a must-have.

There are other ratios out there, so shop around and see if there are any special programs for which you qualify. For instance, military veterans can qualify with a ratio of 41/41.

That's the basic conventional bank financing and mortgage broker lending practice. There are a hundred different ways to do something with all the variables so you need to investigate which programs are available and the guidelines used to decide eligibility.

Owner financing is almost always a good deal if you can get it because you usually can put less money down. The transaction costs are lower, and owners don't ask you to go through the process of being qualified like an organized financial organization would. No more ratios to deal with.

Owner-finance deals are usually used when the property for some reason can't be financed any other way or when the owner has a lot of equity in the property but doesn't need all the cash that would come as a result of a lender paying them off at closing. The seller can be the bank and get a good interest rate on their private mortgage to you while avoiding large capital gains tax. Ask the sellers if they would like to be the bank. Be sure to use an attorney for the contract.

Private lenders are also a good source of funds. Sometimes they are called hard-money lenders because they charge higher interest rates but they won't qualify you to death. Paperwork is minimized and things can move swiftly. Once again, use an attorney to review and approve any private deals.

Family members, uncles, aunts, parents, or grandparents are often willing to help with the down payment money that banks require. Family can sign a letter saying the money is a gift, not a loan, if in fact it is not a loan. Otherwise, it gets factored into that 36 percent back ratio as a loan.

You could also go around the above by becoming joint owners, thus you rely on them to provide credit and down payment money. Buy them out later by refinancing in a year or so, or whenever it becomes possible. Another option is to pay them off when you sell.

Here are some things not to do when preparing to take out a loan. Don't go out and buy a new car, new furniture, a boat, or charge up your credit cards. That is revolving debt on a pay-per-month plan and that can sink you when it is applied toward your qualifying ratios. Wait until after you have closed on the property before you acquire any more liability for debt repayment.

Special note on credit cards: This can hurt you and you wouldn't even know it. Say you have four credit cards with spending limits of $5,000 apiece in available credit. You're a smart person, however, so you have zero balances on all of them. You owe nothing, but the lender says, "Hey, you could go into debt for $20,000 overnight just by taking cash advances." They might indicate that $10,000 is as much potential debt as they would like to see. You would best be served by reducing your total ability to assume revolving debt overnight to a $10,000 limit. You can always reopen those accounts later, if you wish.

The more cash you can personally put into a deal, the more favorably lenders will look upon you. You may be offered lower interest rates or higher qualifying ratios—maybe even a toaster. If you can put down at least 20 percent of the value of the house when you buy it, you will get a lower mortgage payment and the bank will have its margin of safety without your having to pay for mortgage insurance.

If you don't bring with you a lot of cash, you may need private mortgage insurance (PMI). This is an ugly product you pay for to protect the lender. It works like this: Let's say you were able to put down 3 percent to purchase a property but you didn't make your payments like you promised in your lender's mortgage note. The bank can foreclose and take back your property, and sell it quickly for 80 percent of its true value. Since you have given them only 3 percent down, they would lose money on the deal. Your PMI policy, however, makes up the 17 percent difference. (Don't confuse PMI with homeowner's insurance.)

You might also speak to your lender about getting a first and second mortgage on the property as a way of avoiding private mortgage insurance.

● Pros, Cons, and Types of Mortgages

15- or 30-Year Fixed

A standard 30-year mortgage is often easier to qualify for since your payments are lower, but in the long run you're going to pay a lot more interest to your lender. If that's all you can qualify for, take it because you can still shorten the duration of your loan by paying extra money toward the principal when you can afford to. Always ask if there are any prepayment penalties. These clauses prevent you from accelerating your mortgage or rather, paying it off faster than the lender wants, without paying a penalty. Most of these clauses have been outlawed but they do exist. After all, if you sold your house before the 30 years were up, they could penalize you for early repayment. That clause was and is a bad deal. Don't accept it!

The 15-year mortgage saves you 15 years of payments but it takes more income to qualify for it and your monthly payments are higher. Besides, unlike the 30-year mortgage, you can't extend it by paying less. You must make your payments as agreed. Usually you will get 1/8 of a percentage point lower on your interest rate because the lender has the shorter period of risk exposure of 15 years instead of 30.

Adjustable or Fixed Rate

Adjustable interest rates can go up or down. They are always lower than fixed rate loans in the beginning because the lender has the power to raise them if the Federal Reserve raises its loan rate to the bank. Thus you're betting that interest rates won't go up and you're getting a cheaper percentage rate for the risk you take in choosing that option.

Fixed rates in today's rock-bottom interest rate market seem to be the best way to go. You still must decide for yourself. As for me, I'm locking in my right to pay 5 percent or 6 percent forever. These are great rates. Back in the inflationary 1980s, interest rates climbed above 17 percent. I'll stick with my fixed 6 percent, thank you very much.

Once again, there must be 50 different versions of interest rate programs. Those are what can be called blended rates, so make your best deal according to what is currently available.

If you're not sure which way to go or don't quite understand rates and mortgages, go get a book on the subject and read all about it. The lenders will also educate you on what's available in the market at the time, that they can offer.

This stuff is boring to the right-brained extrovert but it is a fact of life and an important one too. When it comes to financing, bear down on it and get through it. Make sure you do your best because you're going to have to live with the end results of your efforts or refinance later and pay more fees.

All through my book, you will notice I don't use all kinds of hypothetical math equations to get my point across. The reasons for that are at least fourfold. First, I'm right-brained. Second, real estate finance books can resemble phone books. Third, all the time you spend understanding some wild finance method is generally wasted because you won't use it in your life, in real estate. Fourth, it's dry as cat litter and it's no fun to read about math.

I can't be all things to all people, so I do not pretend to be a mathematician. I think a little like Henry Ford, who said, "If I need specialized knowledge on any subject, I can push a button on my desk and have an expert give me the best possible answer, which could be formulated or given."

Rely on other people to educate you in your weak areas. We all have them. Simply call upon an expert in your field of weakness. Learn from them while they save you costly mistakes at the same time.

Courage, a positive mental attitude, mixed with purpose, passion and a desire to succeed, will skyrocket your chance at success. Perseverance, willpower, and determination are like carbon is to steel.

Don't let anyone be a dream thief to you. Those people are the enemies of success. Shoot them down with Magic Bullets and succeed.

Equity Lines of Credit

What's an equity line? It's like having money in a checking account that you don't get charged interest or pay interest on until you use it. It is a line of credit based on the value of your property minus what you owe.

Here is an example: You have a house that is appraised at $100,000 and you owe $75,000 on the house. That $25,000 is just sitting there doing nothing, since the $100,000 house represents the collateral for the entire $100,000 amount. So you can get a line of credit set up to have access to that $25,000.

If you have a good credit rating, most banks will set this line of credit up at no charge. You will receive an equity line and a set of checks. Now you have instant access to $25,000. All you have to do is write the check. Bingo! Tax-deductible, tax-free money! (Plan for this with your CPA and your lender.)

Now, here is how you are going to use this line. You're not going on vacation. You're not going to the mall. You are only using that money to acquire more income-producing property. Here is a true-life example of one of the ways I used an equity line advantageously.

I bought a fourplex in Clearwater, Florida, for $100,000. As an investor, I was required to make a 20 percent down payment, or $20,000. I financed the closing costs, which came to about $2,000, so I owed approximately $82,000.

I had done my homework and purchased the property for a below-market price. After putting in paint and carpeting, and cleaning up the place, I had a new appraisal done. It came back at $120,000. The difference between the $82,000 owed and the new appraised value equaled $38,000.

I went ahead and set an equity line of credit to access that $38,000. Hint: Try to work with the lenders your appraiser works with. This gives you greater opportunities to get preferred and approved financing based on an accepted appraiser's opinion of value.

Ask your appraiser what lenders accept their appraisals and use those lenders. This is an example of how your investor network can help you get favorable loans and high valuations.

This is important: If your property can generate enough income to pay for your equity line in addition to your original mortgage payment, you are truly using *other people's money* to get ahead!

Here is how my ultimate financial picture looked after it was all done:

Monthly payment on first mortgage of $82,000	$542
Monthly payment on equity line of $38,000	$303
Annual taxes of $1,800 per year divided by 12 months	$150
Annual insurance of $900 per year divided by 12 months	$ 75
Total for monthly PITI (principal/interest/taxes/insurance)	$1,070

The monthly rents for this fourplex were as follows:

Two-bedroom, one-bath unit	$650
One-bedroom, one-bath unit	$475
One-bedroom, one-bath unit	$400
Efficiency unit	$375
Total income per month	$1,900
Minus PITI	($1,070)
Positive cash flow per month	$830

A note here: When the classified ad was put in the paper, it generated 90 calls from people wanting to rent the units. Using my usual method of screening (see Chapter 11), I was able to pick the cream of the crop. Also notice here that I was offering property for rent to three different sectors of the population: those in search of a 2/1, a 1/1, and an efficiency apartment. The average was about 30 inquires each.

Here is something I learned from the above scenario: It is always more difficult to keep long-term tenants in efficiency apartments, since people who rent these tend to be more transient in nature. So I no longer seek to acquire efficiency apartments. It has been my experience, the smaller the units you rent out, the more they tend to attract transient tenants.

Here is the bottom line: I had my $20,000 initial investment back plus $18,000, and the property income was paying for everything and throwing off a profit of $830 of free money every month except for minor maintenance and water, sewer, and trash fees.

I used that equity line of $38,000 to acquire a triplex for $55,000. I spent $15,000 in rehab money to fix it up and sold the triplex in less than one year for $120,000—a $50,000 profit. One of my tenants bought it. I sold the fourplex for $141,500 a year and a half after I bought it.

My equity line grew to $90,000 when I was holding both properties. That is the amazing power of equity lines. Addition, subtraction, multiplication, and division equal real estate math. No algebra required!

When you have good credit and apply all the principles I am telling you, this becomes a repeatable process you can take with you anywhere you go. It's a transportable skill and a teachable one too.

● ● ● ● CAPTURED IDEAS ● ● ● ●

Notes—*insights, ideas, actions to take*

_____

_____

_____

_____

_____

Strategy—*planning for success*

_____

_____

_____

_____

_____

Tactics—*ways to achieve success*

_____

_____

_____

_____

_____

Chapter 9

Selling Your Property Quickly—Without Paying Commission

What? You still don't have an idea worth the $19.95 you paid for this book? Well, let me show you how to sell your real estate investment at top dollar in the shortest possible time—without paying commissions.

This section will load you up with information in a major way. I'm going to start this segment by saying to you that the law of cumulative effect is going to help you sell your property. Dan's law of cumulative effect states that by using previously proven principles to research, acquire, repair, manage, and prepare your property, your job of selling will be easier. It is a compounding of favorable actions that lead to greater success. Let's assume you bought your property at the right price. It was a solid, well-built property in a good location. Odds are you probably improved it to some degree. It may have appreciated in value over the time you held it, and if you're in a growing area, demand for your nice property has grown as well.

According to appraisal theory, there are two primary reasons real estate does not sell: Either it is *priced too high* or it has been *poorly or improperly advertised*—or both.

Think about it. If you had a $100,000 house that was immaculate and all you did was put a sign in the window that said,

"For Sale—$200,000," people would think you were nuts. But if you put a tiny ad in the newspaper that said, "Immaculate $100,000 house for sale, asking $50,000," it would be gone!

You need a balance. The principle of substitution applies, and again that principle states: No one will pay more for something they could get for a lesser amount somewhere else within a mile or so. Those comparables are out there. They are your competition; beat them.

So the first two things you will absolutely have to do is price it right and advertise it properly. Those are prerequisites to your sale!

Here is what I do and it works without fail every single time. From the start, I know I'm not going to have to pay a commission to sell my own property. I bought it without an agent so I will just reverse the procedure and I will now sell it without an agent. With this in mind, I also know I'm not paying a 6 percent sales commission on a $200,000 house, which saves me $12,000 right from the gate over other sellers who are supposedly my competition and *are* using agents!

Let me explain the psychology involved with buying major assets. People who are not used to spending large sums of money or transacting seemingly complicated deals are very fearful of making a major mistake that costs them in a variety of ways— monetary, a loss of self-esteem, appearance of incompetence, or being taken advantage of. No one wants to be looked at as a fool. So the main reason people hesitate to buy something so large is because of fear.

The first thing you are going to do is remove as much fear as you can. Here is how I do it. First, since I have a $12,000 head start, I will use $500 of that to get my own bonafide appraisal by my true-blue networked licensed appraiser. My house is immaculate when he comes to perform his appraisal inspection, so now I have a true sales price that is accurate. Often this appraisal comes in a little higher than what the property is actually worth, but this allows the buyer to negotiate a little and feel good about the purchase.

Next, I will get my own home inspection for approximately $200. I now have a bound report that details any problems I may have missed. I then fix these things, detailing the repairs and keeping the receipts, if any. Note: Buyers will negotiate a lower price if they find defects you should have found or known about beforehand.

Finally, I will provide the buyers with a home warranty, which costs approximately $400, to go with the house when they buy it. So I have spent a grand total of $1,100 dollars to achieve the following: If the buyers are afraid they are paying too much, I show them the appraisal and explain that it is fairly priced and it will appraise properly.

If the buyers are concerned something may be wrong with the house—What are you hiding? What am I missing? What can't I see?—I alleviate those fears by showing them my inspection report and what was wrong and how I fixed it. They can examine the report and call the inspector themselves.

The appraisal you personally call for and use to help you in your sales process will in almost all cases be done for the reasons stated above since a buyer's lending agency most often requires that an approved appraiser on that institution's list be used to perform the lender's appraisal. You may, however, offer the institution's appraiser a copy of your appraisal (when they arrive) to help them justify the sales price on their own through using the comparable sales that your appraiser has provided.

Regarding the home inspection: If you have a professionally done home inspection and have the receipts documenting repairs done, then the buyers may accept your report in lieu of their own. However, if you have left any questions in their mind or their lender has their own institutional list of approved inspectors then another home inspection will be forthcoming. Either way it is a good investment on your part in finding and correcting any defects yourself before the buyers ever have a chance to negotiate a lower price due to your unpreparedness.

So, my dear buyer, what else are you afraid of? Well, they might worry that they'll buy the property and things will start breaking and falling apart. Here is where the home warranty comes in, showing them they are protected after the sale.

● Preparing the Home

In the years you've owned the home, you methodically rehabilitated it with paint, carpet/floor coverings, landscaping, fencing, vanities, faucets, and so forth. You know that you are doing these repairs and improvements with the intent to sell, so you have used neutral colors and earth tones that generally everyone likes. Now your home should show very well when people come to see it, so your preparation is almost done. By organizing the details of your sale up to six months in advance, you can wait for your higher sales price. You won't be in a rush and you won't have to discount your price.

The approach is identical to what we discussed in "A Military Strategy" in Chapter 2. Keep the house sparkling clean, box up all clutter, and stack the boxes neatly down the center of the garage. Clear out closets, remove framed photos from the walls, and get rid of old furniture in a moving sale, which you should organize a couple of months before you move. Be sure to inform moving sale attendees your home will be for sale soon!

Remember, if you use a real estate attorney to handle your sales contracts and related disclosure documents, you can usually have the whole thing done for about $750. On a sale like the one we have been talking about here, you may also offer the same deal to a real estate agent to see if they would be willing to match the attorney's price. By using an attorney, a title company, staying in contact with lenders, and getting your own home inspection and appraisal beforehand, you will find that your sale will go smoother than you might have thought possible. You can save a $12,000 dollar commission if you're willing to do the work by preparing in these proficient ways.

You're smarter than the majority of homeowners; you bought your home with selling in mind. Have faith that you will do an excellent job when you sell. And you will pay no capital gains on your profit unless you have already exceeded your individual lifetime capital gains deduction of $250,000, or $500,000 for married couples.

● Preliminary Marketing List

Have the following items ready to go when you show the property. Put them on the counter or table laid out in the following order:

- ● The appraisal
- ● The inspection report
- ● The home warranty
- ● Property disclosure sheets (including lead paint for properties built before 1979 and sexual predator disclaimer)

  Note: The sexual predator documentation became mandatory as a disclosure item when a young girl named Megan was abducted and killed by a convicted sex offender who resided in the neighborhood her family had moved into. As a result of that incident a new law (Megan's Law) was enacted to require sellers to advise prospective buyers that they can check to see if predators are in the area by contacting local authorities, who have lists of where these felons reside.

  It's basically a disclaimer that says either we know or don't know, but we have told you about it through this disclosure, and it is your responsibility to check if you are concerned.

- ● Copy of your survey
- ● Current title policy
- ● A copy of your warranty deed
- ● Your latest real estate tax statement
- ● Utility bills for the past year
- ● Copies of any deed restrictions and homeowner's association covenants/rules, all home and appliance warranties
- ● A state-specific pest inspection report
- ● Sales contracts
- ● Any permits for past remodels or additions
- ● Information sheets giving complete details of the facts and features of your home, including a digital photo of the house so they remember which one it was

● Have candles lit and serve cookies and cider for a nice touch, play soft music at a low volume throughout the house

These will answer the lion's share of questions and blow fear clear out of the way. Give buyers the power of clarity. Transfer the feeling of power to the buyer. Give them a secure feeling. Make it easy!

Now take another look at the different ways to find real estate deals listed in Chapter 7. When you devise your strategy to market your own real estate, simply get your product in those high-visibility streams and let those buyers who are looking easily find you. Alert your network of headhunters to turn their attention toward finding you a buyer. Of course, you will give them an incentive in the form of a $500 finder's fee.

● Sprucing Up for Selling Fast

If you want to get top dollar in the shortest period of time, you need to spend some time sprucing up your property before you put it up for sale. By now, you should have new paint inside and out in neutral earth-tone colors, new carpet, and vinyl or tile if needed. The yard should be trimmed, cleared, and cleaned, and everything sparkling clean and in working order. Don't overlook cleaning your light source globes, shades, or covers. Also, put high-watt bulbs in wherever possible (but don't exceed the maximum wattage recommendations of the manufacturer). Your blinds and curtains should be clean and wide open so the light can shine through your sparkling clean windows.

Facts and Features Sheet

Now it's time to write the property's facts and features sheet for clarity and maximum impact. What special features does this property have? Note things like gourmet kitchen, garden tub, home office, hardwood floors, tile throughout, in-ground pool, game room, new roof, appliances, extra storage, sunken living room, fireplace, fruit trees, circle drive, fenced yard, and so forth. What is special about this property? Write it down. Why did you buy it? What did you like?

Gather all energy-efficiency rating materials related to the property concerning appliances, added insulation, new hot water heater, solar energy, gas appliances, and so forth.

Describe everything that will remain with the property as part of the sale, such as draperies/window treatments, ceiling fans, chandeliers, vanities, shelving, appliances, garden equipment, sheds, garage door opener and remote controls, and outdoor ornamentals. Also make it very clear what will *not* be included with the sale and put it in writing.

Write down area facts, such as parks and recreation areas, shopping centers, transportation lines, locations of schools, churches, police, and fire.

Now you will take your preliminary marketing list (all your legal paperwork) plus your facts and features data sheets, and design the best property information worksheet you possibly can. Go to www.audrie.com to create your own free facts and features sheet.

Here's a checklist:

- Take a digital color photo of the property or use a traditional print. You can have color copies made at your local copy shop.
- List the street address plus the legal description lot and block (from your deed).
- Include the number of bedrooms, bathrooms, and garage size (one-, two-, or three-car) or carport.
- List the year built, style (i.e., ranch, bi-level, tri-level, two-story), size and square footage of living area, garage, and porches and/or decks.
- List the type of foundation, type of construction (i.e., block, wood frame), type of roof, and heating and/or cooling system.
- List any special features—fenced yard, circle drive, fruit trees, greenhouse, swing set, appliances, home warranty, security system, and so forth. Also include any updates that were made, such as a new kitchen, bath, carpeting, tile, and painting.

● List nearby amenities—parks, schools, churches, shopping, public transportation, fire and police departments, beaches, amusement parks, golf, skiing, and so forth. If the home is in a gated community or a waterfront property, be sure to include that.

● Include deed restrictions, homeowner's associations (and dues amount), and whether public water and sewer is available.

● If your friendly appraiser gave you a high number, try to list your sales price just below that value and say, *"Selling below appraised value* at $199,888." It gets attention!

● Give your phone number to schedule appointments.

Now is a good time to write your newspaper ad since the information is fresh in your mind. Basically, you need to abbreviate into a classified ad what the information sheet details. In addition, you will want to set your open house dates in that ad—usually Saturday or Sunday from noon until 4 P.M. works best.

Important: Always have no fewer than two people present during an open house or showing, and be sure to put all valuables in a secure place.

Before your showing date arrives, make sure you have your yard signs and street corner signs posted at appropriate locations. Intersections included, flags and balloons also attract attention (your call). In the home, have your facts and features sheets, records, including disclosure sheets, warranties, inspection report, appraisal, home warranty brochures, blank contracts, offer sheets, earnest money agreements, and all of the other information available so that you have the answers and the proof when your prospective buyer asks for it (and they will).

Again, as with any contract you sign, make sure you put on it, "Subject to our attorney's approval." Cover yourself! Note: A real estate attorney should be able to provide most of the forms you need if you can't run them down yourself. You can also get free or low-cost forms by visiting www.audrie.com, www.USLegalForms.com, www.kaktus.com, www.UrgentBusiness Forms.com, and many more.

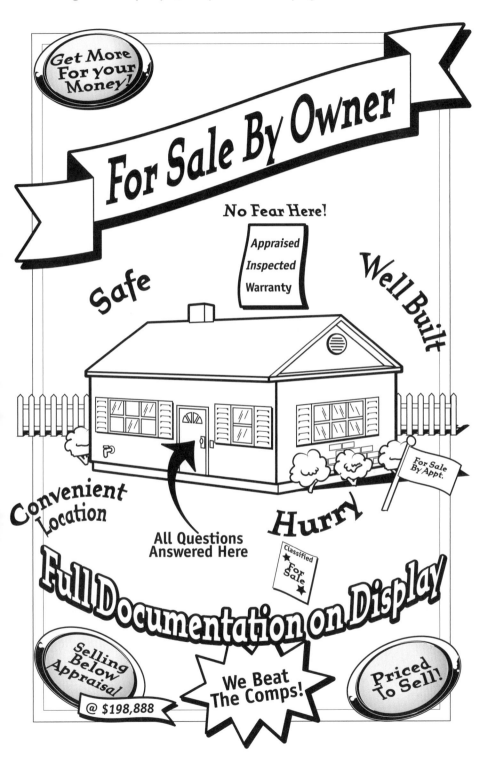

Now that your property is immaculate, appraised, inspected, repaired, under warranty, advertised properly, and priced right, you should be able to find a buyer quickly. And by "quickly," I mean in 45 days or less. You are beating the daylights out of your supposed comparable competition because you've done your homework. Since you're not paying a $12,000 commission, you can offer your buyer more.

When I am selling a property, every buyer in the market knows it's available. In addition to newspaper ads, you can also use yard signs, corner signs, free listing sites on the Internet, brochures, flyers, word of mouth, local thrifty magazines, neighborhood alerts, and other creative ways to gain exposure for your property. The principle of substitution holds true and the laws of cumulative effect all allow me to control the entire process. The reason being, I have worked harder and smarter using information other sellers don't have.

For those who are just getting started in real estate the National Association of Realtors (NAR) has an exclusive information service called the Multiple Listing Service (MLS). This service allows participating real estate brokers and agents access to view all the listings of participating members throughout the country. The major benefit to the home seller is that when working with a real estate broker or agent who has access to this database, that seller will have the benefit of exposing their property to the widest audience of real estate professionals in the country. These professionals in turn will be able to research properties that fit potential buyers' criteria giving the buyers the benefit of knowing what is for sale in the areas of interest to them.

Some information from the MLS is making its way to general public Web sites through various methods throughout the industry. However, many of the powerful tools of this service can only be accessed and used by participating real estate professionals. By visiting www.realtor.com you will see the general public's benefit as a result of this service.

I have in the past accepted phone calls on my property and scheduled a certain day and time other than my open house dates when I have agreed to show my property. Usually, about two days later from when I received the call, I will have received a few more phone calls. I schedule everyone to see it at the same time. This serves two purposes: If someone doesn't show, I'm not standing there, sucking my thumb, waiting for him or her. I will get others who do show up and when they do, the auction atmosphere has been established. I've used this to my advantage before and it resulted in my getting a higher price. Two buyers wanted it and the price went up.

In a nutshell, prepare it, price it right, advertise it properly, and protect your buyer's interests with complete information, orderly forms, and documentation. Remove all fear in the buyer's mind and look for the perfect fit in a buyer.

Similar to screening for tenants, now you're screening for potential buyers. Ask lots of questions and get to the real reasons why someone is interested in buying a property like yours. Real estate brokers and agents would call this a form of prequalifying your buyer. They would also make sure a potential buyer really could afford to buy if they did like it.

Here are some questions you can ask of potential buyers:

- Do you live in the area?
- How long have you been looking?
- How many homes have you looked at?
- Are you in the market for a home right now?
- Do you currently have a home you need to sell?
- Do you plan to buy in the near future?
- Have you spoken to a lender and are you preapproved?

These questions will reveal what type of visitor you are speaking to—whether they are motivated, just looking, a nosy neighbor, qualified, and so forth.

I would like to mention one more thing about pricing your property or anything else for that matter. It is called a price point. Example: If you are looking to sell your property for $250,000, price it at $249,888. If you are at $200,000, price it at $199,888. Or if it's at $150,000, price it at $149,888. Why the $888? You may say, "I'm used to seeing $999." Everybody takes $1 off to drop down to the next lower bracket, but you are smarter than that. You are making it look like this number is a specific odd amount that needs to be realized from the sale. I have found that people hesitate to bargain as much and they tend to remember the home better because of the odd sales price. You've got to be smarter than the average bear, Yogi!

● ● ● ● CAPTURED IDEAS ● ● ● ●

Notes—*insights, ideas, actions to take*

_____

_____

_____

_____

_____

Strategy—*planning for success*

_____

_____

_____

_____

Tactics—*ways to achieve success*

_____

_____

_____

_____

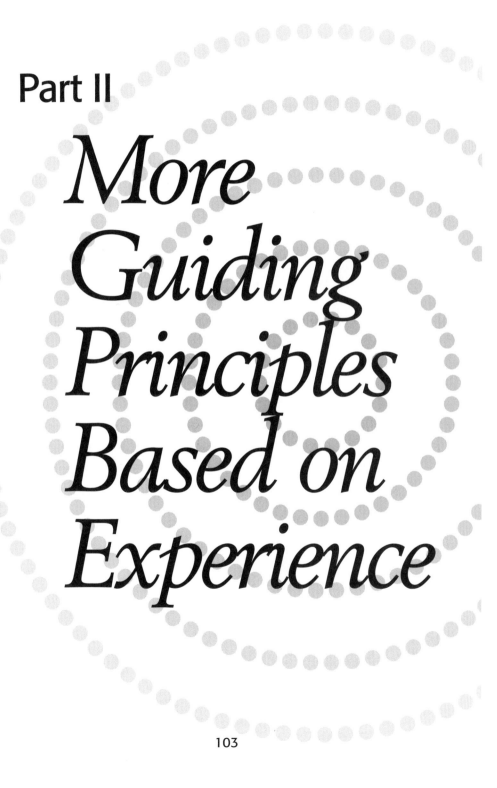

Part II

More Guiding Principles Based on Experience

Chapter 10

Appraisal Basics

Very simply put, an appraisal is an opinion of value; however, that opinion is derived by taking any of three different approaches to arrive at a justified opinion of value: the income approach, the comparable approach, or the cost approach.

The following is a simplified example, but it demonstrates each. The income approach is generated by figuring out what a property will generate in annual income, minus vacancies and collection losses. If, for example, you have a $200,000 duplex as a rental, the income approach may be used to determine value. Assuming no vacancies or collection losses, multiply $200,000 times 10 percent (capitalization rate) = $20,000, divided by 12 months = $1,666.66, divided by 2 units = $833.33 per unit per month. If you want a general ballpark figure to calculate a possible price based on rent, you might use this formula to help you figure your return based on different rental and cap rates. Don't forget your mortgage, taxes, insurance, maintenance, utilities, assessments, and other costs. After all expenses, you have a yield, or profit.

The comparable approach is most often used in single-family home valuation. The appraiser takes three or more houses that are similar in style, size, quality, age, and neighborhood—preferably within a mile of each other—that have sold within the last six months to one year. Adjustments are made for better or worse features to the comparables to arrive at a probable sales price of the house that is being appraised. This approach is based on the principle of substitution, which says no one would pay more for something they could get for a lesser amount somewhere else (within a 1-mile radius).

The cost approach takes into account all factors involved in duplicating the exact copy of what exists currently or replacement cost of constructing something that is similar in utility, plus a few more factors. The bottom line is how much would it cost to build that building on that site today?

Here is a golden nugget for you: Take a real estate appraisal course. If you do this, it will catapult your real estate investment career. I guarantee you will gain more insight into real estate by doing this one thing than just about anything else you could possibly do. The perspective and information you will gain from a few weekend-long classes are priceless. You will gain vision, ideas, and understanding. You will have an edge over every other investor who has not done it.

I was lucky enough to be taught by an instructor named Steven V. and he is truly a genius. This guy could make millions if he applied himself to real estate investment but he chooses to teach and give back to others in that way. He is very comfortable in life, and money is a byproduct for Steven.

When I finished the class, I had appraisers wanting to hire me to go to work. Of course, I don't want to work as an appraiser. I just want to think like one and that is why I took that four-weekend course. That class taught me more than both of my real estate licensing courses combined. The reason for that is real estate classes deal with state laws, contracts, regulations, and ethics. Appraisal focuses on evaluating real estate and that is what you want to learn as an investor.

I've said it before: You don't need to go to college for four years and you don't need a real estate license to be successful in real estate. What you do need is a guy like me to convince you to go to appraisal school and read books like the one in your hands right now.

When it comes to real estate, the appraiser looks at buildings and land differently than the rest of us humans. There are some things we mere mortals can understand and those are quality, functionality, aesthetic appeal, and location.

Appraisers have six quality scales and they read like this: low, fair, average, good, very good, and excellent. The way they see it, finished wood floors are better than carpet; tile is better than vinyl; hardwood cabinets are better than particle board; bricks are better than siding; ceramic is often better than plastic or vinyl; solid wood doors are better than hollow core; high-energy-rated double-pane windows are better than single pane; and so forth. It's the quality and the degree of difficulty to construct something that give high marks for condition. Square footage of living space, factory floor, or showroom space play a very large part as well. (Note: Most nicer middle-class dwellings score an average or good on the appraisal scale.)

These are things to think about when looking at property as an investment. Is it made of quality materials and is it well constructed? Does the building measure up to code on plumbing, heating, electric, roof, foundation, structure, and present use in zoning? Is it built to last, or is it going to fall apart and wear out and break down sooner than it should? Is it energy efficient or will it cost a fortune to operate? Is there a demand for this type of real estate? How scarce or plentiful is this investment? What do future economic indicators forecast is in store relative to current conditions? Does it look better or worse? Hint: Think about social and economic trends and circumstances. Some insights about location and growth patterns are in order here too.

● Short Story About Location

There once was a man who wanted to buy some investment property, so what he did was *look at growth patterns*. You should do this too, by going to your city's *planning and zoning department*. You can see growth patterns and you definitely want to buy property that stands in the way of growth.

This is how he used what he learned. He saw that city planners had decided that a new artery (highway) would benefit their city by creating linkage to another city about 100 miles away, so being a smart investor he only went as far as a ten mile limit to be able to be close to his investment.

Now on average, new growth will radiate out from existing prosperous cities in the direction it is planned at a rate of about one mile per year. So our smart investor had a plan to cash out in about 10–12 years.

What he did was buy 10 acres of commercially zoned property very cheaply because there was no demand at the time. He bought it, fenced it in, put up some lights and a gate, and held onto that little bugger. Now that new highway was coming his way and the good folks, through their taxes, were paying to have it built.

It didn't take long for the heavy equipment to start cutting a swath toward his fenced-in storage facility and when they got close enough to him, he started renting out a secure area for everything from road cones to generators to backhoes. You name it—it was stored there. This more than paid off his land.

Now the men and their equipment eventually moved on further down the trail but they left a finished highway behind them. And guess what? Lo and behold, people started driving on it, and then started buying property to build houses to get away from the city. Since the new highway was a straight shot into town, ten miles out was a breeze.

Well, of course, here comes the herd and everyone is just populating the whole darned area. And within ten years, residential housing surrounds Mr. Investor, and can you guess what he's got? Yep, a prime piece of commercial property, 10 acres large.

So in accordance with his 10–12 year plan, he sells his storage facility to make room for the new office/business park complex for more than $2,000,000. That, my friend, is *vision,* and the sooner you get a clear picture of what it is that you want to specialize in, the sooner you can retire to the islands.

Okay, story time's over. Let's get back to work.

● Location

Buy in the way of growth! For residential housing needs, you're looking for proximity to schools, shopping, fire station, police, bus lines, major access roads, hospitals, and general service industries. These mean safety, security, and convenience.

Important to location for commercial property is access to major roads and proximity to large population centers, as well as police and fire protection.

As for industrial location, you may look for major highways, railways, airports, and waterways. Transportation routes are a key factor for industrial production and distribution. Police and fire protection are also a security concern that needs to be met to some degree.

With regard to all locations, watch out for hazardous materials dumping grounds. You don't want to get stuck with an EPA nightmare!

If you take the time to go to your city's planning and zoning department, you will get an education you cannot buy. It is a very valuable information resource. Here you will get the big picture of the environment in which you will seek your gains. You can ask lots of questions, and the astonishing truth is this city department actually has answers. It has aerial views, demographic statistics, annual population growth rates, pictures representing new areas of development, new planned highway projects—you name it. This office is as close as you get to having a crystal ball in predicting the future of your city or town.

Again, buy in the way of growth. Growing cities generally grow 1 mile outward each year, which can be determined through planned growth patterns.

When you are searching for residential property, keep these time-tested and recognized patterns and trends in mind. Neighborhoods that are all rentals don't appreciate (go up in value) as fast as owner-occupied residential neighborhoods do. If you can find or create a good rental property in a neighborhood of owner-occupied homes, it will be more valuable.

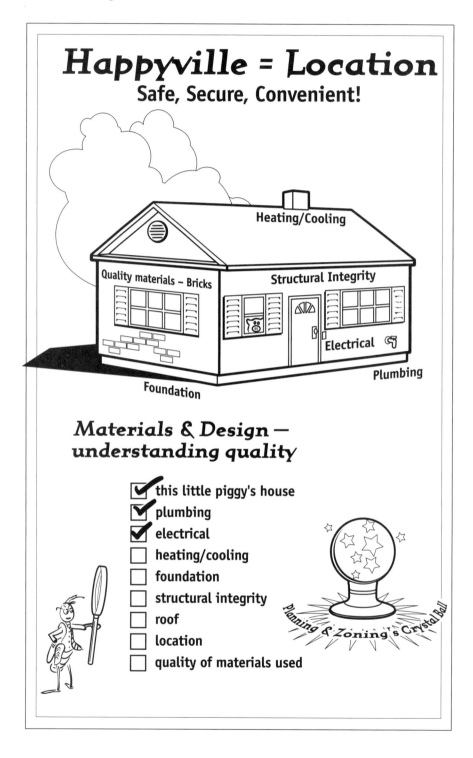

Happyville = Location
Safe, Secure, Convenient!

Heating/Cooling

Quality materials – Bricks

Structural Integrity

Electrical

Plumbing

Foundation

Materials & Design — understanding quality

- ☑ this little piggy's house
- ☑ plumbing
- ☑ electrical
- ☐ heating/cooling
- ☐ foundation
- ☐ structural integrity
- ☐ roof
- ☐ location
- ☐ quality of materials used

Planning & Zoning's Crystal Ball

Neighborhoods change. Here's how to recognize what phase they are in. Generally, there are four phases of life in real estate.

1. Growth. In a new young neighborhood, you will see lots of tricycles and children's toys, swing sets, and so forth (on the tree of life, the outer bands of city centers).

2. Stability. The neighborhood is established. Now you see basketball hoops and bicycles; the kids are older and use two wheels to get around.

3. Decline. Demand is diminished as the kids are gone and now the parents are riding their own three-wheel bikes. People pass away and the houses become dated and run down. This depressed market cycle has opportunities for buying rehab properties.

4. Revitalization. Renewal, redevelopment, and modernization create new demand. One tip here: Assess neighborhood conditions at three different times—morning, noon, and night. Look for high traffic, hoodlums, noise, and/or congestion. You want peace and quiet, safety, security, and convenience 24 hours a day, seven days a week.

Hint: As a result of your buying the houses that need fixing up at the phase three stage (decline), you help to create the forth stage (revitalization). Your greatest potential to find quality fixer-uppers is found in neighborhoods that are in phase three life cycles. Remember, tricycles to bicycles to three-wheeled bikes, then renewal and the tricycles come back out again!

● ● ● ● CAPTURED IDEAS ● ● ● ●

Notes—*insights, ideas, actions to take*

_____

_____

_____

_____

_____

_____

Strategy—*planning for success*

_____

_____

_____

_____

_____

_____

Tactics—*ways to achieve success*

_____

_____

_____

_____

_____

_____

Chapter 11

Finding Tenants 101

● Be a Landlord, Not a Slumlord!

I live by the following "landlord's creed":

**I vow never to rent to someone else, something
that I myself would not be happy living in.
Mansions not included!**

You will have a much better life if you live by that creed.
Your tenants will appreciate you, and you will automatically be
driven to the point of understanding how your tenant feels about
the place they are going to be calling home.

Never—*never*—neglect, mistreat, or abuse your tenants. In
fact, I sometimes think I treat my tenants better than I treat my
friends. I respect and value them; I appreciate and care about
them. I really am concerned about their well-being and security.
If they call me with a problem, I send someone right out or I go
myself to correct it. If *I* were without hot water at home, I would
have it fixed within 24 hours. I look at the problem through my
creed and believe me, I feel good when their problem is fixed.
My service technician is also a good spy; they report back to me
any other potential problems within.

So you say, "But, Dan, how do I get these heaven-sent tenants?" Well, *the law of cumulative effect* has a lot to do with a
smooth operating investment and here's how it goes.

113

You did your homework in the beginning by understanding how to evaluate a good property in a good location and buying it at the right price. So to begin with, you have a desirable rental that is mostly trouble-free, that you can rent out to good people at a fair price, and thereby increase your position in life by adding happiness and contentment to the lives of others.

You may be thinking, "I've invested so much time, effort, and money. How can I be sure I won't get the tenants from hell?" Here's how you are going to find your dream tenants.

Assuming your property is absolutely ready for someone to begin living their life in, you are going to place a real estate ad announcing to the community that you are accepting applications and will be interviewing prospective tenants. Note: Applications and credit checks come after people have seen the property and after you have interviewed and seen them. Don't spend your time or others' time on paperwork until you have a tenant who fits initial screening criteria.

Always keep in mind when designing your advertisement the following acronym: AIDA. You want to get people's *attention, interest, desire,* and *action.* What benefits do you offer? What is the advantage of leasing from you? Make your ad stand out, with a headline and a border if possible. Get people to see your rental first, before they get tired of looking and settle for something less!

Pattern your ad after this:

> For lease—3-bedroom, 2-bath, 2-car attached garage; 1,800 sq. ft. ranch style home w/split plan; central heat/air, all appliances, fenced yard; immaculate condition, new carpet, tile, paint; close to Adams Ave. and U.S. 19; 1st, last, security; $1,350 a mo., WSG included. Call 555-1212 for appt.

Let me break this ad down for you. It is going to perform some very specific functions for you.

● *For lease.* Use the word "lease" instead of rent; a lease says to people, "This is a long-term commitment. I should take these people seriously."

● *3-bedroom, 2-bath, 2-car attached garage*—Spell out what you are offering.

● *1,800 sq. ft. ranch style home w/split plan*—Now you're telling them how much room it has for all their stuff, and they begin to picture a long, ranch-style home that has privacy.

● *Central heat/air, all appliances, fenced yard*—You're telling them it is comfortable and comes well equipped to serve their needs. The fenced yard adds security and privacy.

● *Immaculate condition, new carpet, tile, paint*—Here you are telling them you care about your property and don't lease to slobs. You also care about your tenant, so you have given them the luxury of new carpet, tile, and paint. You are also subtly saying that there is nothing wrong with this house. Your tenant won't have any problems, and they are expected to appreciate and take care of your investment.

● *Close to Adams Ave. and U.S. 19*—Give people major landmarks so they know where the property is generally located. Don't put the exact address in the ad. You do not want people driving by, knocking on the door, disturbing neighbors, or barging in. This is a crucial part of the screening process. Your carefully worded ad should appear in all editions, north, south, east, and west. You want maximum first-time exposure in the most popular, largest circulation newspaper in your city or town.

● *1st, last, security; $1,350 a mo., WSG included. Call 555-1212 for appt.*—This is the bottom line: $1,350 a month + a month + another half month as a security deposit. This is telling people to do the math. Is it out of your price range? We do pay for your water, sewer, and garbage. $1,350 + $1,350 + $675 = $3,375 cash required before you sign our lease and take control of our hard-won investment. We mean business! We will not accept a check at this meeting; you must bring cash! (Note: Cash is required for immediate occupancy; otherwise a cashier's check or personal check that clears before the tenant gains occupancy or gets the keys.)

Now I can almost guarantee if you have done everything right up to this point, your phone is going to start ringing as soon as the paper hits the street. I encourage you not to answer it. This is why: You are in control. You are going to let the answering machine get that call, with a message that says, "We will be returning calls after 5 P.M. today. Please leave your name, number, and a brief message. Thank you." Why do this? You are going to listen to those people on the phone. You're going to get a feeling for who they are and the validity of their reasons for wanting to rent your home.

Do not discriminate based on age, race, religion, national origin, sex, or any of that garbage. It is against the law and you are potentially ruling out an excellent tenant. What you are looking for is the person who has the perfect and most logical reasons for wanting to lease what you have. Plain and simple—you're looking for the best fit. Based on that criteria, start calling people back.

Here is a good screening script I developed to get to the core issues quickly:

1. Why do you want to lease as opposed to buy?
2. What do you feel our house has to offer that others don't?
3. Where do you live now? How long have you been there?
4. Why are you moving?
5. When do you plan to move?
6. How long do you think you might stay here?
7. We require first, last, and a half-month security in the form of cash and a one-year lease. Can you satisfy these requirements? (Do not bend—establish control early!)
8. Please allow me to call you back. I'll have to talk to my spouse (or partner).

That was your prescreening interview. You can now begin calling people back again as a result of taking notes while you used the above script. As you screened each caller using the script you should have written down their name and number again while assigning a best-to-worst rank, say 1 for excellent and 10 for worst. You took those notes to review and determine who appears to have the most valid reasons for wanting to lease your rental.

Now call your most promising prospective tenants back first, and tell them you will show the property at noon on Saturday. Continue down your list, scheduling showings at 1, 2, 3, 4, and 5 P.M. Now, these people don't know you have scheduled five other appointments on Saturday and a few more on Sunday but they will after you have shown the property to them.

As soon as your potential renter shows up to view your property, take note. Are they on time? Can they keep their first promise to you? Can they follow directions?

If they are late, did they get lost? I'm sure you gave them good directions and also used landmarks like churches, stores, or monuments, so they could find you easily. If they can't follow simple directions, do you think a lease agreement and those directions are going to be any easier?

Say they did show up on time. This says they respect your time, are able to follow directions, and are serious about finding a nice place to live.

How did they arrive? On foot, bike, bus, cab, truck, motorcycle, or tractor trailer? Preferably they arrived in a clean, well-kept passenger car in good condition. It runs fine so you won't have cars on blocks and a parts yard for a front lawn in six months when they buy more cheap junk to get around with.

So the car looks okay on the outside—but how about the interior? Do they smoke and have garbage everywhere? Does this vehicle look like a home on wheels, with garbage bags filled with clothes, a crying baby, and a cat in the back window? Watch out if you see this type of telltale evidence. I don't think I need to paint the picture of what will result if you miss this investigative step.

Pickup trucks with camper shells can also be loaded to the gunnels with personal effects, including small zoo animals. I encourage you to get a look back there, too!

The bottom line here is people will generally treat your property the way they treat their own—if you're lucky!

How are the appearances of the folks? Are they clean and well groomed? Do they seem to fit the profile of what you had envisioned during the phone interviews? Have they successfully fooled you or deceived you into believing something else up to this point? Now that they have appeared before you, is it evident whether or not these persons are con artists?

If you get an uneasy feeling within the first few minutes of meeting these people, don't brush it off as just some crazy thought. That's your self-preservation instinct operating and you'd better listen to it.

Sounds easy enough, doesn't it? Yet so many people screw this process up. They also make mistakes by choosing management companies to do this highly developed type of intuitive researched and planned-for event. I honestly know of no management companies that can be as thorough as an owner who takes the time to protect their own interests in this way.

I don't care how much management companies protest about the above statement. The fact of the matter is, they are not you, so they can never find a tenant that satisfies your own personal preferences the way you can.

With the way I approach real estate, it is 100 percent guaranteed every single time that I am going to outsmart, outwit, outperform, over-deliver and under-promise to the point that I crush my competition. I am in a league of my own. You need to be too.

My tenants are the winners and they know it, too. What kind of loyalty do you think develops in the minds of people who look to me for protection? It stands as a testimony and irrefutable, self-evident, empirical fact that I care enough about the people who have entrusted me with their welfare, their time, their money, and their trust to deliver on my promises. My tenants don't move. They either pass away because of old age or they end up buying it from me when I want to sell it. It happens that way all the time.

So think again when you hear a dummy landlord talking about all the trouble they had and then ask yourself one question. Did they read *Magic Bullets* before they became a landlord? It's 100 percent certain they did not. If they had, their tenants would have loved them and paid for their real estate time and again, and made them wealthy in a variety of ways.

Back to your prospective tenants: They might just say this will do. We will take it right now. Here is where you tell them that you cannot do that right this moment because you have promised to show the property to other prospective tenants who are interested in it as well. Politely inform them that you will be calling all parties back after 6 P.M. to inform them of your decision. If you have done it right, you will be calling the perfectly fitted tenant back at 6 P.M. on the dot, to inform them of their good fortune in being chosen as the best tenant. Remember, you are in control!

Once you are sure these tenants appear to fulfill your requirements, ask them to go the rest of the distance by filling out your rental application and allowing you to run the infamous credit check. A non-refundable application fee of $25 is standard at this point.

I have always used the lease agreements straight out of the *Landlording Manual* by Leigh Robinson. If I want to add any further terms and/or conditions, I create an addendum and include it with my lease. I make master copies and keep them on file. If you have any questions, I suggest you consult that new attorney you found to help you.

A neat trick here is to go to a real estate office and pick up a rental application to use as a template to create your own personalized application. For credit checks, follow the directions located at www.MrLandlord.com or www.thelpa.com.

Once everything checks out with the chosen tenants, call the other folks back and inform them that unfortunately, you are very sorry but another applicant was chosen. Keep backup tenants just in case your first choice falls through.

Congratulations to you and your tenants. You both win if you have the perfect fit.

Give your tenant a signed copy of the lease and a set of keys to their new leased home. Give them your contact information and some self-addressed envelopes to send in their rent checks. Be attentive and care about these wonderful people.

● Mind-Reading for Landlords

The better you understand your tenants and their personal situation, the better you can serve their needs and your own. Notice that your needs come after your tenants'. Always put your tenants' needs before your own and they will buy real estate for you in return. That's a fair trade. Take it!

Many cold-hearted, self-serving, money-grubbing, wanna-be landlords don't understand human nature. Let me tell you right now—if you can't put yourself in another person's shoes and see a problem from that person's perspective with empathy, you will fail miserably in the "landlording" business and in life. Wise up!

Fear not. If you're not quite sure what I'm talking about, here come the stories and details of how to be loved and adored by those kind people called tenants.

Let me first dispel the horror stories about landlording. If you follow my advice and teachings, you should have few tales of woe to tell. You've heard the stories and they sound like this: Those darn, lowlife tenants. They trashed our house, disturbed the neighbors, ruined our lawn—they were filthy pigs who never paid the rent on time and it cost us a fortune to get rid of them and repair our investment.

Well, guess who's fault that is? Yep, it is completely and unequivocally the fault of the so-called person who is calling him- or herself a landlord. The real name for this type of so-called landlord is "uneducated dummy" and because of these lazy fools the whole industry gets a bad rap!

There is a plus side to the scenario above and that is this: It sets up a perfect opportunity for you to do the exact opposite of the fools and create for yourself an unlimited market supply of excellent, trouble-free tenants for life!

Tenants, believe it or not, are human beings. They are not animals or things to be mistreated, abused, or taken advantage of. If you prepare your rentals as if your mother were going to be moving in, your mind-set will be realigned in short order. In effect, you will start looking at it from a compassionate point of view. You will not cut corners. You won't let things go that need fixing. You will use care and diligence in preparing that dwelling for another human being to begin calling home. You want to provide a trouble-free, pleasurable, aesthetically pleasing, creature comfortable, needs-fulfilling, safe, secure, affordable, and convenient place to live. When you provide those things and screen the population, it's like striking gold.

A word of caution: Watch out for real estate investment property that comes with existing tenants. In general, the new owner takes the property subject to the existing lease and rights of the tenant or tenants. Most often, whatever existing lease or rental agreement that was made with the previous owner will remain in effect.

What could happen if you don't thoroughly review existing tenants' lease agreements? What if the previous owner rented a unit to his good-for-nothing, drug-addicted brother for $1 a month for the next five years? That's a valid lease. You may take the seller to court for misrepresentation but it's going to cost you lost rent and lost sleep—and maybe your safety. So be sure not to overlook this important step.

Here's another example of an intentionally designed below-market rent lease agreement. Let's say you're getting a great deal and you buy it. Then you find out the reason the owner sold it to you was because the tenants were difficult and had him over a barrel. All the while, they are paying lower than average rents and complaining about everything. Now you get them and you can't raise the rent and they refuse to move. Here comes your eviction lawyer and you have attorney's fees and more lost rent to boot.

My point is this: Make the seller get rid of bad tenants before you close on the deal. Do a preclosing inspection and personally walk through the empty apartment, house, or condo yourself. Bring extra locks or call a locksmith and have the locks changed the day before closing. An honest seller will not have a problem with that so long as the title company holds those keys until your check is accepted at the closing table.

When you install new tenants, you are generally going to get a higher rent from the property because inflation creeps along and landlords have a hard time raising rents on people. I have seen 10- to 15-year long-term tenants paying the same price for 15 years. You will go broke if you let that happen. Adjust your rents accordingly every time you fill a vacant unit, and if people want to renew their leases, then inform them of an economic reality that currently exists called inflation, and you are just keeping up with it. The Annual Consumer Price Index may be used as a reference. If they don't understand, they have an option and that would be to go look for a similar rental to yours at a lower price. If you have followed my advice, this elusive lower rental price will not be found and your tenants will be grateful to you for renting out such a clean place at the new price-adjusted rate.

Although we mentioned earlier that 1 percent of a home's value is often a good starting point for setting rent, you can also figure out how to set your rent by checking the classifieds. Use the Sunday classified ads to find four rentals similar to yours in size, location, and amenities. Add the four rentals' combined rents together and divide by four to get the average. Set your rent 10 dollars below that average; on average, you will have the lowest rent. This will likely result in having the majority of people who are looking call you first. Now you can pick the cream of the crop using the script I gave you earlier.

There is a lot of garbage held out for rent, and prices may be lower, but few people want to live in a pigsty with lime-green shag carpet and orange countertops, where the roaches tell *you* what to do.

So the lesson here: Encourage balking tenants to find something comparable to yours at a lower price. If they find it, let them go. Odds are, they won't. After all I told you, it's often next to impossible if you're a hands-on owner. There is no 10 percent fee to management companies either. So you can even ask 5 percent less than investors who use professional management to do their job. So many ways to slaughter your competition —so little time!

● ● ● ● CAPTURED IDEAS ● ● ● ●

Notes—*insights, ideas, actions to take*

_____

_____

_____

_____

Strategy—*planning for success*

_____

_____

_____

_____

Tactics—*ways to achieve success*

_____

_____

_____

_____

Chapter 12

Guide to Leases
With Option to Buy

What's the deal with the "I buy houses" signs and ads that we see all the time? In many cases, those are investors hunting for motivated sellers who may be willing to sell their real estate using a method that says, "If you will lease your property to me with the option to buy it or lease-option it to another buyer, then I may be able to help you get out of this situation with your credit, your sanity, and a few dollars in your pocket to boot."

The key to these investors' achieving success is in finding very motivated sellers who are nearing foreclosure, have little equity, or generally need to be free from the burden their property represents. As a result, you will see investors advertising for motivated sellers using the "I buy houses" signs and newspaper ads. They also call the FSBOs, and other for sale or for rent properties in hopes of coming across a motivated or flexible seller who may consider their plan.

The flip side of their strategy is to also advertise for people looking to buy homes on the easy credit plan, which in effect is the old rent-to-own program. You've seen the ads: "No credit? No problem! Bankruptcy, divorce, that's okay. We can help." The two factors necessary for the program to succeed are (1) they must find motivated sellers who will sell to them using an assignable lease with option-to-buy contract, and (2) they must find the eager tenant-buyer who they can sell the house to using their own rent-to-own with lease option-to-buy contract.

These investors are in some sense of the word, middlemen. They match eager sellers with eager buyers and structure the deal in their best interests. The more desperate and willing these two parties are, the higher the profit potential for the investor.

Let's look at some of the advantages and disadvantages to the three parties who are involved—the sellers, the buyers, and the investors.

Advantages to the motivated seller may be that they get out of a property that is months behind in mortgage payments or that has no equity. They may get a fair offer at a current market price that will be paid in the future. They can move on with their lives and save themselves all the hassle involved with trying to sell the property and save their credit rating as well.

Disadvantages to the motivated seller are that they most often are left responsible for their original loan while the investor controls the property. They often lose a fair amount of equity and all of the future appreciation value during the lease-option period, while being bound into contracts that give the investor maximum control of the deal's details in the form of binding agreements. The seller is also at risk of getting the house back at the end of the option period if the housing market has crashed.

Advantages to the tenant-buyers are that they can begin to acquire a sense of ownership by renting to own with small amounts of their rent going toward a future down payment if they choose to exercise their option to buy. Also, they don't have to qualify using traditional lending guidelines, and they can walk away at the end of their option's expiration date if they decide not to buy.

Disadvantages to the tenant-buyers are that they have to deposit on average a 5 percent nonrefundable option fee. On a $150,000 house, that would be $7,500 forfeited if they do not follow all of the rules, can't qualify, or choose not to exercise the option when due. They will often pay above-average rent for the option privilege and any rent credits would also be forfeited if the option is not exercised. They are also expected to make all minor repairs while often being charged an above-current market price if they do buy, while at the same time receiving none of the tax advantages during the lease-option period.

Some of the advantages to the investor are that they limit their personal liability to the lenders as they keep the seller's original financing in place using subject-to clauses. They ask sellers to carry back what equity they do have by using low-interest private balloon mortgages, interest-only loans, graduated payment schedules, and a host of other creative methods that are often in favor of the investor not paying until cashing out in the future when the property is sold. Often the seller is negotiated down to a rock-bottom price and the buyers are charged a much higher future value price, which is based on assumption of certain market conditions continuing.

In addition to the above advantages, if the real estate market bottoms out, the investor has the option to give the property back to the original owners at their option's expiration and let them take the loss. The deals are also often structured to capture all future appreciation and equity accrued through mortgage reduction, only paying the seller a set amount that represents their current equity with no further added benefits. If the tenant-buyers don't exercise their option to buy, then the investor is entitled to keep all of the money that has been paid up to that point. The investor then finds a new tenant buyer and repeats the process, only this time they may have an opportunity to charge more due to the fact that the home may have appreciated in value.

One more note: Because the investor requires the tenant-buyer to be responsible for all minor maintenance and repairs and holds the original owner responsible for any major repairs, they also avoid the proverbial landlord trap of getting called in to repair all the things that can go wrong with homes throughout their holding period.

So as a final note regarding advantages to the investor, the lease with option to buy with right of assignment contract allows the investor the choice of whether to rent the property, sell it for a quick profit, or sell it on the longer term rent-to-own program, thereby maximizing their total investments return.

Disadvantages to the investor are, if they are not diligent in researching a property and its true ownership, they can waste a lot of time and effort, and they may have an eviction to process if the tenant-buyers default, as well as repairs to make if damage occurs. The investor has to have ironclad contracts to ensure their legal rights are protected and can be defended in court. They also must sift through a lot of sellers and buyers to make profitable deals work!

Why would buyers and sellers buy from or sell to a lease-optioning investor? My personal opinion is because they are desperate or have been ill informed in a variety of ways. I could go on here to tell you how to proceed concerning lease-option deals but to be perfectly honest, it goes against my nature to, in many cases, take advantage of certain people's ignorance that leads to the investors being able to profit off of other people's desperate circumstances, even if they did do it to themselves! I am well aware I will hear it from all sides concerning my comments here but those who take offense at my observations may be exactly the individuals I seek to expose. Let me also say that in many cases, these investors are providing a valuable service to those people they save from foreclosure. They also help those people who otherwise may not have been able to purchase a home. So there is merit in the ethical investor's existence, and they are not the bad guy when they act with care and concern for those people who trust them to truly provide a fair and equitable solution to their immediate needs.

If you would like to pursue the lease option game, then by all means get the books, tapes, and contracts; go to seminars; and find a mentor with high ethical standards to safely teach you how to do it right. I see nothing wrong with it *if* you are ethical and truly are out to treat other people fairly while seeking no unfair advantages. By acting in that manner you will be providing a very valuable service and should be paid accordingly.

Just ask yourself this question before you proceed to contract on a lease option: "Would I want someone else to act toward me the way that I intend to proceed with them?" Let your conscience be your guide and you should be able to enjoy your profits as a result of all your hard work. Go to www.Lease2 Purchase.com for details.

● ● ● ● CAPTURED IDEAS ● ● ● ●

Notes—*insights, ideas, actions to take*

_____

_____

_____

_____

_____

Strategy—*planning for success*

_____

_____

_____

_____

Tactics—*ways to achieve success*

_____

_____

_____

_____

Chapter 13

The Fine Art of Negotiation

Negotiation as defined in the dictionary means, "a conferring, discussing, or bargaining to reach agreement."

That definition is somewhat vague and offers no real insight into how to be effective when you attempt to employ it to your best advantage. How else can we describe negotiation in general? To transact, bargain, confer over, haggle, barter, cope, handle, deal with, or manage; these words describe the act but leave a lot to be desired as to how one actually does it!

Let's say that negotiation is a basic means of getting what we want from other people. The ultimate solution is to let other people believe that your ideas are their own. If you can achieve that, it only stands to reason that there can't be any arguments as a result.

In real estate, the person who appears most desperate will in most cases lose the advantage in negotiation. That of course explains why every real estate buyer looks for motivated sellers, since it naturally builds in advantages to the buyer's benefit. Sellers who can wait to get their price, effectively reverse this process or at the very least defend against it.

It is a known fact that when you can build on a relationship that is based on creating mutual benefits, you will tend to encounter less anger and resentment that can kill your deal. One way to ease into the negotiation process to your benefit is to be well informed with facts, figures, data, and information. This will help you present your case forcefully without personally attacking your opposing party. Use hard facts but be soft on feelings, using tact and thoughtfulness to understand the other person's needs as well as your own. This doesn't mean that when someone plays hardball with you, you are going to be a push-over. It means you are considerate while remaining firm.

Age-old wisdom tells us that when you attempt to solve prob-lems, the more options and creative alternatives you can present, the better your odds of achieving a successful result. Informa-tion is power so you need to be bold and ask a lot of sometimes personal questions if you are going to solve problems effectively. As an investor you should always maintain a position that al-lows you to walk away from a deal if the other party's proposals or counteroffers become unreasonable. Your odds of greater suc-cess are multiplied when the other party needs the deal to go through more than you do.

Negotiation is an art and a science. Just like everything else, it takes practice to become good at it. Another important point in negotiation that you cannot afford to overlook is to under-stand who you will be dealing with throughout the process!

Is your competition fair, honest, trustworthy? Is he or she a person of their word? Is he or she sophisticated, experienced, or more knowledgeable than you? Is this person a crafty, schem-ing, double-dealing opportunists who lacks credibility, integrity, character, and a sense of fair play? There are many variables to consider and you are often put on the spot early in your rela-tions to come to an accurate evaluation in your own mind of just what type of individual you are currently attempting to deal with. Often we rely upon our instincts to provide us with a general awareness of character, however a crafty individual can achieve remarkable acts of deceit toward those who do not prac-tice deceiving others like it's a full-time job.

It has been said that there are three types of characters who circulate in our midst. They are not as easy to spot as you may think, so let's take a look at them, shall we? The following is a brief description of each.

Character 1 is the type person who, right from the start, lets you know where they stand. They tell you what they want, what they'll do, and how they intend on doing it. They are up front, direct, and to the point. Most often these individuals are not shy in telling you they are out to get everything they came for, so you are officially put on notice that you are dealing with a person who doesn't pull any punches.

Character 2 is the type who politely listens to what you propose to offer and appears to be willing to compromise and negotiate with you for mutual benefit. They gain your trust and let the deal proceed as though it will be a win-win situation for both of you. But in the end, they take advantage of the false sense of security they have deceived you into believing while still getting the better end of the deal and leaving you to wonder how you got suckered into believing otherwise.

Character 3 is the type who appears to be a kind, caring, and considerate soul who only wants to see that you are taken care of at all costs. They appear to want to help you get all the benefits while they would be happy with just some small token of gratitude for their help in getting you what you want. But again, in the end, they too want all they can get from the deal, even if it means appropriating your funds to their checking account's bottom line.

What does this say about people and whom you should choose to negotiate or conduct business with? We all have our own best interests at heart; it is a self-preservation instinct that hearkens back to the time of the cavemen. But rather than brute force, today's weapons of choice are language, contracts, and persuasion.

There is only one real choice here and that is to choose character type 1. They are not out to deceive you, and they don't surprise you by trying to take things you thought you had agreed on or things you thought they never wanted in the first place! Character 1 puts you on notice from the moment you meet them that he or she will be straightforward in what they want, how they proceed, and what they expect as a result. At least this individual gives you an accurate representation of who he or she is and what to expect. There will be no surprises. You can conduct your affairs knowing you *will* get your "just compensation" as you had planned it because the person has no deception in representing themselves to you.

All professional investors prefer to deal with straightforward, knowledgeable people when they conduct business. Things work smoothly and each of the parties attains the intended benefits that were bargained for. There is no attempt to get something for nothing or take unfair advantage of someone else's inability to properly defend themselves.

I make it a personal mission to try to protect the disadvantaged from the wolves. I hope you will too, when you see an opportunity to defend those you can.

● Prepare to Negotiate

Keep the following in mind:

● Know what you want by beginning with the end result in mind.

● Have as much information and data as possible beforehand— *facts, not feelings.*

● Be open-minded and flexible.

● Set minimum and maximum limits on what you will accept beforehand.

● Be familiar with and ensure you understand every word on contracts before you sign them.

● Never appear desperate or sign anything under pressure; be a friend of time.

● Always have an "out" and be prepared to walk away from a bad deal.

● Seek to create mutual benefits while limiting anger and resentment.

● Try to separate the people from the problem; focus on interests, not positions.

● Know what type character you are dealing with before you begin.

● Have a system, program, or plan in place that helps you establish and maintain a fair amount of control.

● Try to offer less and ask for more at the beginning, thereby leaving room to negotiate and concede small concessions later.

● Follow up as needed after the ink has dried to limit or prevent buyer or seller remorse and rights of rescission from being exercised. Don't let your deal unravel.

Prepare to win! The more organized and informed you are beforehand, the more likely you will achieve a more beneficial result in your own behalf.

As a final measure of protection—and I have mentioned this before—there is one magic phrase that can be used to protect yourself from possible mistakes or strong-arm tactics and deception: *This entire agreement is subject to my attorney's approval.*

Wolves absolutely hate it when you use that phrase, so use it at the end of all your agreements just before you sign on the dotted line. You will protect your own interests effectively when dealing with others.

● ● ● ● CAPTURED IDEAS ● ● ● ●

Notes—*insights, ideas, actions to take*

_____

_____

_____

_____

_____

_____

Strategy—*planning for success*

_____

_____

_____

_____

_____

Tactics—*ways to achieve success*

_____

_____

_____

_____

_____

Chapter 14

Complete Home Rehab in 10 Days

This chapter assumes that you have already or will soon acquire a house that is ripe for rehab. Be selective and sure of the house's potential to allow for a profit after all the hard work is done. I will help you find your house or houses.

It helps if you choose a house that already has a sound plumbing, heating, and electrical system. These are things that are expensive to correct in relation to the value they return to you upon resale. Most often, people cannot see the inner workings of these systems and they take them for granted.

Very few buyers are going to give you an extra $15,000 to $20,000 in your asking price because you have replaced things that they can't see and already take for granted as just a basic component that is buried in the structure. Also, they assume these components to be warranted against defects by you. After all, it is mandatory in most, if not all, states that you fill out a disclosure form informing the buyer of every defect that exists or ever has to your knowledge. So, inspect the systems of your investment alternatives carefully, since they can be expensive to repair and replace, with minimum dollar return value being realized at the sale.

Along these same lines, you should also pay close attention to the following cash vacuums:

● Roof
● Foundation
● Structural integrity

Here are a few ways to quickly gauge a home from its appearance: Stand across the street from it. Now look at the bones of the structure. Does it look like a swaybacked horse, with the roof sagging in the middle? Does it have flat areas in its design that don't allow water to be drained away quickly?

Water, dampness, and rot are the equivalent of cancer to the human body when it concerns a structure. Shingles can be replaced—that won't necessarily stop me from buying. Usually I will use that old roof as a bargaining chip in negotiating the seller down to a lower price. However, if I crawl into the attic and see that the plywood has become rotted and truss members are also affected, it's time to move on to my next potential deal. Life is too short and I will never rehab it in 10 days if I have to rip the roof off and rebuild it too.

Some other conditions, such as sagging eves, wavy roof surface, rotten fascia and trim pieces, and insect infestations can be deal killers too, if severe.

Solution: Get into the structural members with a long, sharp, sturdy, standard flat-tip screwdriver and attempt to penetrate structural components that are made of wood. You won't hurt anything if there are no underlying deficiencies. However, if someone has freshly painted over or patched it, that screwdriver is one heck of a lie detector! Use it. (Now, I'm not saying people would do that. It may just be the termites have eaten everything but the exterior coating of the wood to conceal their activity.)

There are also tile roofs, metal roofs, cedar shake roofs, concrete tile roofs, hot-rolled roofing, tar and gravel roofs, and always a few new high-tech roof coatings. My main concern is whether the decking or the roof support structure has been undermined by water, insects, rodents, poor materials, poor design or craftsmanship, a lack of fasteners, strapping, and so forth. Shingles and coatings can be replaced. Just know what is underneath. Negotiate lower for needed replacement of roof coverings if you can. I dwell on roofs because it protects everything else!

Next on the list of deal killers is the foundation. Again, stand back from it and look at it from a distance. Does this place look like the Leaning Tower of Pisa? Are the seams coming apart? Do the windows and doors look square? Are porches, stairs, and additions on firm ground as well?

Block homes can tell you very quickly if they are stressed out just by the appearance of the mortar joints. Those giant unsettling cracks tell a story. This does happen and may not be cause for serious alarm since those cracks may have occurred 10 years ago. Be sure to get a qualified inspector's opinion if further investigation is warranted.

Once again, water is a sign of trouble with foundations because it leads to erosion, rot, mold, and mildew. It washes out foundation materials and slabs will crack. It rots sill plates and your walls are no longer firmly attached to a base.

If the house has a crawl space, it's time to put on your coveralls and investigate. Before you enter a dark, supposedly uninhabited, infrequently entered, dark area, assess the situation. Ask someone who has knowledge of the dwelling if there has been any animal activity they know of. You may encounter bees, wasps, ants, spiders, snakes, slugs, mosquitoes, rats, mice, and a host of other inhabitants. Beware and be prepared. It's truly another world in some cases. If you don't want to do it, hire a licensed, professional home inspector to protect yourself in all areas if you're just not sure!

Okay, you're a trooper and you're going in. Good for you, Rambo! You'll make it in this business because it takes faith, guts, and determination. By getting into this type of situation, you'll learn a lot more about every part of the homes you inspect.

You should have a strong flashlight, your trusty screwdriver, maybe some insect repellent and a safety observer standing at the access entry to give you peace of mind. Now you can go to the perimeter walls and inspect where the walls meet the foundation. Look for rot, misalignment, cracks, separations, water damage, or any other condition that doesn't appear normal.

While you're down there, look at the other foundational supports. You will see pier blocks and posts, other concrete support pillars and walls, beams, joists and cross bracing, and the underside of subflooring. Check this stuff's condition. Does it look original? Is it structurally sound? Or are there some discrepancies that need further investigation? Take a good look and smell!

Don't leave yet. You will want to look at all that plumbing and electrical there as well. Scan the perimeter. Do you see any sunlight coming in where it shouldn't be? That might be a hole that needs repair. Simply follow everything to its logical end, looking mainly at the condition of the different components.

Okay, you've made mental and physical notes. Now dust yourself off and go inside the house if everything has checked out so far.

So the roof and foundation have passed your keen eye. Let's look at the rest of the house with respect to its structural integrity. More than half of your structural integrity check at this point is already complete since the roof and foundation are two of the most important components and those have been done. Now you are left with the interior spaces of the structure.

Here's what I do once inside. I stand at the front door with a checklist in hand (see www.InspectAmerica.com for a free checklist) and I begin to scan the walls, ceiling, and floors. I'm looking for water stains on all three surfaces, as well as patches that were used to repair or conceal damage. I go through every room and look for signs of damage or concealment.

Any flat floor is a good candidate for my scientific marble test. I'll drop my marble; if it rolls to a corner, that floor ain't level. That's a simple test but I do want to know that the underlayer or subflooring is sound and firmly attached to all those joists, beams, and trimmers.

Soft spongy floors are of concern, creaky floors are annoying, and rotten floors are another story. So once again, I'm looking at the structural support of the floors. I don't care that the cheap, yellowed vinyl is coming up at the seams. I don't care that the carpet is matted down or threadbare, and I don't mind if the finish is worn off of hardwood floors, or tiles are loose. Floor coverings fall under the label of cosmetics. That's such a pretty word and that's what you want to concentrate on—cosmetics. More on that in a moment.

So the floors pass my test for subflooring and structural integrity is great. Now I can check that the walls are square because they are attached to that floor, and then I can check that the doors all operate properly and are square too.

"How much more can there be than that, Dan?" you ask. Well, let me tell you a few things that can bite you here. Let's say the structure overall is good. By that, I mean you have a solid roof, a solid foundation, and sturdy floors and walls.

What is behind those walls? The things that bite you aren't usually seen until you get bit. One particular painful bite is finding out your wiring is not grounded or that the circuits are not properly protected. You're looking for three-pronged outlets and modern plastic-encased wiring made of copper, not aluminum. You want circuit breakers, not fuses. What you really need here is a licensed electrician to do this more in-depth and professionally licensed review of the system.

I have seen more than one Joe Homeowner rehab go up in flames because of a lack of respect for electricity. Licensed electricians bring you up to code and protect your investment. Find a good one and make it a point to shower him or her with praise, attention, and money.

They will give you free estimates, so use them as a preliminary inspector with you. If you decide to buy it, use them to do the work that needs to be done.

Plumbers are a breed apart. You would think they use gold for soldering your pipes with the prices they charge. A plumber may or may not give you a free estimate. With a little digging, it can be done. Just give them the work if indeed you do buy the house. With plumbers, the only time you're going to need one is if you are doing major system work or the once-every-10-year hot water heater job. Then of course there is the occasional clogged main sewer line to the street.

In today's PVC plastic plumbing kits world, you can hire just about any good all-around handyman to get the job done. If you have to tear through a wall to get at plumbing, the building code inspector-man will say, "Get a licensed plumber."

If the house you're inspecting doesn't have adequate heating and cooling, that can become expensive. Let's say you have a flat-roof home in a hot climate with window-unit air-conditioners, and you intend on bringing this house up to what a modern-day home dweller expects. You may have a problem. Where would you put new ductwork if you don't have attic space to house and route central heat and air? Once again, call in a pro if you need some advice. They do give free estimates!

Here's a point for you to follow up on: The plumbing, heating, and air-conditioning guys all drive service trucks. Be on the lookout for those trucks. If they are your neighbors, introduce yourself. Many of these guys do work on the side—and that means half price. You may have to pull a permit as a homeowner but the savings are substantial. Develop a network of these blue-collar geniuses. They are the guys who will transform your investment fast!

So now you have a solid house. Plumbing, electrical, heating and air-conditioning, roof, foundation, and overall good structural integrity are in shape. So what's left to do? Call in your army of carpenter ants—painters, flooring installers, yard maintenance workers, tree trimmers, and handymen of all sorts. Let the demolition guy in first. Order a dumpster for the next 10 days. Instruct the demolition man to throw out everything *including* the kitchen sink. What I am out to do at this point is to clear the decks.

A blank canvas is created for the painters to perform the transformation. They come in at this point and patch and paint. Let them blast the place with their airless paint-spraying arsenal inside and out. Give them three days and you have just added a huge improvement to your investment. This is the biggest dollar-for-dollar return you can make.

One cautionary note here: Make absolutely sure that quality paint is used. When it comes to painting, it's the labor that kills you, not the material. I insist on Sherwin-Williams Super Paint. It is a miracle formula that I am convinced could cover up bullet holes without any patching compound and it lasts forever. It's worth every penny!

Once the painters leave, the flooring guys are right behind them, laying tile and carpet. These guys are out in two or three days, and the cabinet expert and plumber are called in next. Light fixtures, vanities, toilets, sinks, doors, switch plates, outlet covers—all are replaced. Ten days are up and this house is either held out for rent, lease-optioned, or sold for a whole heck of a lot more than the $10,000—if that much—I just put into it.

It takes time to recruit your cosmetologists, but you will run across them in your travels. Friends and family usually can provide you with some good leads. Start networking and talking to tradesmen. Get their numbers and schedule them to descend upon your ugly duckling at certain times and watch the transformation begin. If you don't know anyone, ask a local appraiser to suggest who he or she would use.

It took me a long time to learn these tricks. For years, I did it all myself and it took me at least three months. The sad part is that I thought I was saving money that way.

Can you see how much I actually lost? Here is a quick example: I bought a house for $55,000. Its deficiencies were purely cosmetic. I used other people to do all the work and I pitched in to keep them organized. Ten days later, it was done. I spent a total of $5,000 on materials and labor and it appraised at $90,000 in 10 days!

That's $30,000 in 10 days—not 3 months.

There is no doubt about it. You can do it. It may take you a bit longer the first few times, but soon you'll gain the experience I have. (You're gaining it right now—use it!)

● ● ● ● CAPTURED IDEAS ● ● ● ●

Notes—*insights, ideas, actions to take*

_____

_____

_____

_____

_____

Strategy—*planning for success*

_____

_____

_____

_____

_____

Tactics—*ways to achieve success*

_____

_____

_____

_____

_____

Chapter 15

Your Own
Home's Improvement

If you're looking to improve your own home, here's an overview of how you can create a more effective and successful project—whether you are doing it yourself or working with a contractor.

Let me begin by saying what a home improvement plan will *not* do. A home improvement project, addition, upgrade, remodel, or makeover will not make up for a troubled marriage. So for those that think home improvement may save a marriage, I'm telling you now that it will add more stress and it is a poor substitute for proper counseling.

With that said, when you see a home being sold because of divorce, take a good look at the house because you may see evidence of a great remodel job. However, the marriage still failed. The scenario above leads into other areas of home remodel, acquisition, and selling points. Gentlemen, pay attention here! It is generally recognized that women are responsible for 80 percent of all decisions on whether or not to purchase a particular home.

So what influences women in their decisions concerning home purchases and remodeling? By far the two biggest are the kitchen and the bath. If I had to choose one or the other, I believe I would look at which area was in need of the remodel more, while at the same time looking at the costs of both options.

As for the men, what do they want? Most would be happy with a large garage/workshop plus a secluded den or office to carry on with business or to retreat to the solitude of a "cave. Generally speaking, men don't pay much attention to draperies, window treatments, flower boxes, state-of-the art appliances, Jacuzzi tubs, well-lit bathrooms, large closets, or floral patterns of any kind. They often prefer brown and gray *everything*, big garages, a shed, a sprinkler system, and a fenced backyard for barbeques and lounging in private. Men also like low-maintenance houses.

Those are general observations and many times they will not apply. However, by keeping them in mind and using the 80/20 rule, they may help in the decision-making process. So now using what we know, it would be wise to slant your remodel toward the feminine side of life.

Let's look at the kitchen first. Can you paint or refinish the cabinetry and change the knobs and handles to get a new look? Would new Formica laminate over the old countertops with a matching backsplash do the trick? Maybe a white ceramic sink with a new faucet will achieve the desired effect? Quite possibly you may decide to rip it all out. If that is the case, then paint the walls and consider tiling the floor also. Often adding some minor electrical and lighting upgrades will help transform and modernize the entire effort. Don't forget the new built-in dishwasher and plumbing as well.

Custom cabinets, if designed, built, and installed by a local reputable cabinetmaker with references and a picture book of previous work done, are often very attractive in price and quality. I use craftsmen with low overhead who work on one job at a time. Often I will ask them to make, in addition to the kitchen, a base cabinet for the bathroom to match, all for one low price. When working with kitchens I always look to see if a wall can be opened up to create a pass-through or barstool countertop. This lets in more light and allows the person in the kitchen to talk with and see the people in the adjoining room. It also creates the effect of a more spacious kitchen.

The bottom line is that a well-lit, light, bright, and spacious kitchen, well equipped with modern appliances, plenty of storage space, and decorative tiles, paint, and window treatments will add value and appeal to any home's remodel plan.

Next, let's look at remodeling the bathroom. Here again, we look to the feminine side as women often spend more time here than the men. I will often bite the bullet and rip it all out, the tub being the only exception. If I can leave the tub in, the job is easier, faster, and cheaper. However, if I am looking at an olive green or yellowed, chipped rusting ceramic eyesore, then a new fiberglass insert with a sliding glass door is going on my list of items to buy at the local Home Depot.

Jet tubs are the in thing, so I won't rule them out as a possible upgrade. This decision again is based on the female since most males don't take candlelit bubble baths or require a pulsating massage. Walls are painted with Sherwin-Williams semigloss paint, which creates an excellent moisture barrier to the walls. With regard to walls, by adding tile or laminate half-wall wainscoting to the lower three-to-four feet of the wall, you'll add a nice touch. Since you have torn out the old toilet and base cabinet, now is also the perfect time to rip up the old vinyl and put down ceramic floor tile before the new fixtures are installed.

New lighting, mirrored vanity cabinets, ground fault circuit interrupters (GFI—required by code) electrical outlets, wallpaper borders, and towel bars are usually the finishing touch. Even a man can appreciate coming home to a spacious, clean, modern, functional, and aesthetically pleasing kitchen and bath. One final note here: Be sure to caulk everything when you're through. You'll want to protect your new investment from rotting from the inside out. Dampness and wood-eating insects are your home's worst enemies.

Now with the kitchen and bath out of the way, what do you feel is next? I myself spend on average about seven hours a day in the bedroom, so I tend to go there next. Once again, the closet is important, so I will paint that bright white, upgrade the lighting, and install a closet organizing system to maximize the space that is available. You might also consider putting in a shoe rack.

Once the closet is done, I patch and paint the rest of the room. I always make sure I get enough paint to do the ceiling as well. Once the walls and ceiling are done, the ceiling-fan-with-light kit and dimmer switch go in. Then the baseboards are prepared for installation before the carpet goes down. Usually I paint the baseboards a shade darker than the walls and tack them to the wall about a half inch above the floor.

Now that the paint is put away, it's time to install the plush carpet and a dense quality pad beneath it. In order to really bring the room together, you will need to take a paint swatch or chip to the carpet dealer to choose the carpet color that really sets off the walls and baseboard trim. Final touches include mini blinds, curtains, and decorative switch plates and receptacle covers. A solid-core door with a keyed lock set for security represents today's modern standards, so I will add that factor in too. Just add candles and you're done!

As for the rest of the house, I will choose one color of paint and use it throughout all the remaining areas that are to be lightened and brightened. Earth tone, eggshell, tan, or sand colors—such as Navajo white—are a neutral favorite of many, so unless you have a floor that is going to clash with it, earth tones are a safe bet. Speaking of floors, I will follow appraisal rules that tell me wood is better than carpet, except in bedrooms. And tile is better than vinyl. With that in mind, I will use tile and Pergo flooring everywhere else. Once the tile and wood are installed, I never have to replace them and maintenance is a breeze.

There you have it! A general Joe Homeowner remodel job.

● Adding Square Footage

But what about the infamous addition? With this consideration, you'll have many more options to weigh, so let's take a look at some of the pros and cons of adding square footage:

1. Is it physically possible, legally permissible, and financially feasible? Will the new addition serve your intended purpose to the maximum extent?

2. Does the current floor plan, layout, or design of your home allow for a smooth flowing traffic pattern in, out, and through the proposed addition?

3. Will your lot size accommodate a larger dwelling and will the neighborhood surrounding your home support the higher value you expect?

4. How long do you intend to stay in the house for which you've planned the upgrade? Five years from now, will the addition net you additional money on your sales price, dollar for dollar?

5. Are you prepared to deal with draftsmen and plans development, contractors, building officials, and permits? Will you mind living on a construction site for about six months? Are your finances in place, with an additional 10 percent set aside for cost overruns? Has everyone agreed on what this addition should look like and the purpose it will serve?

Let us say you have considered the above and would like to continue toward the improvement. From here, we should consider the economic principle of what is called *progression*. For example: You have a two-bedroom, one-bath home located in a neighborhood of more expensive three-bedroom, two-bath homes. In this case you could, with more certainty, add another bedroom and bath and expect to be able to realize or achieve the value from the addition's expense as the more expensive homes around you will tend to pull the value of your home up along with theirs.

But the reverse is also true, so you must consider the opposite case that is called the principle of *regression*. If you over-improve beyond the value of the homes that are surrounding you, then those lower value homes will tend to keep the value of your home in the lower price ranges. You can only improve so much before you reach a point where, for every dollar you spend, you will receive less of that same dollar back when you sell.

A good rule of thumb to use is to try to get at least $2 of increased value for every dollar you spend. Once you begin to approach the break-even point, then you should consider maintaining what you have as opposed to adding to it. A simple way to say it: Don't over-improve!

Another term to be aware of is super-adequacy. That would be like putting gold faucets in a mobile home. It's overkill and too high end for the property's overall value, so the final decision on remodeling and additions comes down to balance and reaching a happy medium. Also take into consideration the cost; aggravation; net gain; need for improvement; improved quality of life; suitability to all occupants' tastes, needs, and desires; and the ability to ultimately receive a higher sales price.

I choose to remodel more often than add on because it goes much faster and the profits roll in more quickly. If I need more space to live in, I simply remodel the house I'm in and rent it out for top dollar, then get an equity line to buy a bigger house! When remodeling my own home, I attempt to do everything myself, aside from building cabinets or rewiring electrical circuits. As with everything else, if I get in over my head, I will concede defeat and call in an expert to finish what I started while I learn where I went wrong by watching them finish it up.

If you decide to add a room or two, you can save about 30 percent of the total cost by being your own contractor. There is a book by Richard M. Scutella and Dave Haberle titled *How to Plan, Contract, and Build Your Own Home* that will give you a proper grounding on the subject. If you feel up to the task, get a book—there are many different titles out there—and be vigilant. In the end, you will have that new addition at a significantly lower price.

Here are a few parting shots.

Painting everything inside and out is the greatest value-producing improvement you can make on a dollar-for-dollar return basis. When painting, ensure you buy the absolute best paint available, since it is true that the expense of painting lies in the application of the paint not the paint itself. So if you have to apply two coats because of an inferior, watered-down paint, the cost just doubled in time and the added paint needed to get the job done.

Another thing you can do to improve your home substantially is landscape it. Landscaping, if done right, can add up to 20 percent to the value of your home. I prefer to plant shrubbery and low-maintenance hardy plants and trees. Plant some flowers to add color and you're finished.

● ● ● ● CAPTURED IDEAS ● ● ● ●

Notes—*insights, ideas, actions to take*

_____

_____

_____

_____

Strategy—*planning for success*

_____

_____

_____

_____

Tactics—*ways to achieve success*

_____

_____

_____

_____

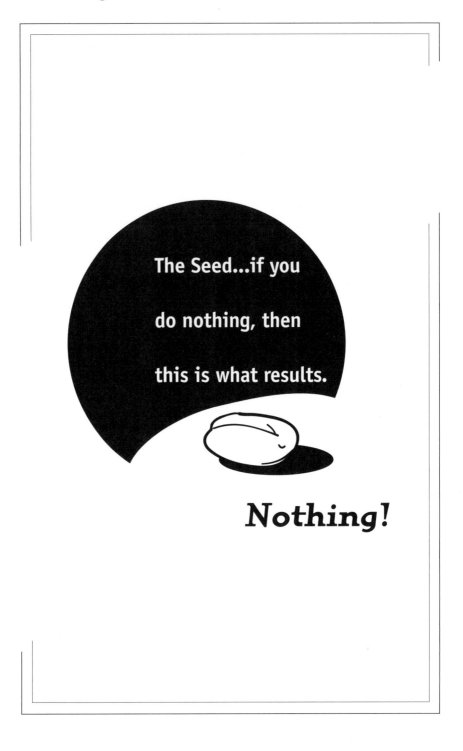

Chapter 16

A Real Estate Stock Plan

This chapter will attempt to weigh the pros and cons of active real estate investment versus passive stock investment alternatives. Let me first begin by saying one word to you: Enron. Well, what did you expect? Yes, this chapter is pro real estate, con stocks. How appropriate!

This chapter will not contain any high-tech, gobbledygook, stock market charts, graphs, trends, analyst picks, projections, company reports, or insider tips. In real estate, you personally have the power to develop and create all of those things yourself. I could never trust other people's secondhand opinions or publicly disseminated information to get the jump on the herd.

If I were a company officer, or majority voting shareowner, or a paid agent of those individuals, I might think differently for the simple fact that I am getting the jump and could make some *dinero* if I know something the majority does not. Overall, people are told to build companies so they can sell it to the public through offering pieces of their company to the public in the form of stock. So I know from the very beginning that the owners of companies are selling me a piece of paper they say is worth a certain amount of whatever value a dollar is worth at that time.

Let me see if I understand this. I transfer my hard-earned cash and I pay a fee and/or commission to do this, and you give me a fancy certificate and a promise that this represents a solid investment decision. No way!

I've seen people lose their life savings counting on other people's paper promises. I am not comfortable sitting on the sidelines rooting for everyone else to make money for me. Who are we kidding? I would be last in line to get paid after all of them. And just how are they getting paid? Well, I see it as this: They get me to buy more fancy certificate paper, backed by more promises, while at the same time encouraging me to hold onto the previous certificates. All the while, the value in those is slowly liquidated to pay salaries and expenses of the inside corporate raiders of my blind faith and trust.

Yes, I am a skeptic. Let me shift gears here and take back everything I just said because frequently what I just said is dead wrong and two words will prove me wrong quite often. Those two words are "Blue Chips." Many companies do provide value, dividends, and growth opportunities. Who am I to talk bad about the stock market? Don't get me wrong. It's an awesome institution and a complex and intricate financial function of the world's economy. Everyone feels the effects of this juggernaut and many people are afraid to upset the world powers by saying anything that will get the ire up of the kings of Wall Street, so they just clam up and slump into obscurity.

To heck with that attitude! Take control, people. Actively manage your own hard assets and get off your butt and quit rooting for the other guys out there to make money for you.

Use your brain to directly control the events that are going to add to the bottom line. With real estate, you can use relatively simple math and your two eyes to see the whole picture. No charts, graphs, prospectuses, opinions, or guesstimates. You invest less than 10 miles from home in your own neighborhoods so you know all about market activity and current local economic conditions. You know prices and demand for your investment, since the local classified section of your newspaper is an instant picture of your market's fundamental outlook. Your competition advertises its position and you react immediately.

I buy my houses below market price, add value to them in a hundred different ways, and capitalize on those assets. It's hands-on direct control. There's no guessing, no hoping, no cheering, no scanning for loopholes in incomprehensible legalese boilerplate.

I circulate, select, and direct. I negotiate and use my own strategies and tactics. I rehab valuable hard assets and use them to generate income, build equity, access tax-free cash, shelter other income from taxation, and lower my tax brackets. Almost everything in my real estate business is deductible, so my gains are my gains. I can defer paying gains with 1031 exchanges and a host of other legal and ethical, easily understood ways to secure my future profit picture. You don't need a license to do this, just a pulse.

A note on 1031 exchanges is in order here: 1031 exchanges allow you to exchange like property held for business or investment purposes, thereby delaying immediate capital gains taxes. The result is that you have more money to reinvest now.

The following are four things you must do when using the 1031 exchange rule:

1. Identify a new property within 45 days of your sale (or prior to the sale).

2. Close on your new property within 180 days.

3. All the proceeds from the initial sale must be reinvested.

4. The new property must be of a like kind, held for business or investment. (Your tax attorney or accountant can guide you through.)

If you feel real estate investing is more difficult than stock market investing, I believe you are wrong. It's much safer for the average individual who doesn't have all kinds of crazy options, puts, and calls, true insider tip-offs or hours and hours of time to hopefully understand more than the next guy in order to sell your stock to the next person for more than you paid for it. Unless you're accredited, you should be institutionalized.

With real estate, if I buy my investment property with owner occupied, 10 percent down financing, I am using 90 percent loan-to-value leverage. I don't suggest you do that in the stock market. If you make a little timing error, your investment career could be over.

So to put it in general terms, $1,000 controls $10,000 and $10,000 controls $100,000. If I buy a house that costs $100,000 and I put $10,000 down to control it and the market appreciates 10 percent the first year, I get my $10,000 back and keep the asset. It becomes a perpetual money machine and I don't have any of my own money at risk.

There are closing costs but they are deductible as expenses. Here is another point. My rich Uncle Sam wants me to provide housing for his citizens to live in, so he lets me take depreciation on my investments to encourage me to rent them out to others. This explains a tax benefit in real estate that helps us common people who actively participate in the management of the investment and who are not making over $150,000 a year in adjusted gross income.

For example, if you pay $100,000 for a house, Uncle Sam says this house will slowly disintegrate to dust in 27.5 years—39 years for nonresidential property. (Of course many homes are hundreds of years old. Many of those have been renovated, rehabilitated, remodeled, and properly maintained. Others that have had no maintenance or care are long gone. The government takes the approach that if nothing is done, the dwelling would be worth zero at the end of 27.5 years, with only the land value remaining.) The land will always remain, 20 percent of the purchase price is considered land. So you only depreciate the house's value. In this case, that would be $80,000 and $80,000 divided by 27.5 years = $2,909.09 per year for 27.5 years. That benefit can get you in lower tax brackets by reducing your taxable income on other income, such as your regular job or other investments.

Thus, you save today's dollars, and when you sell the house years later Uncle Sam recaptures that amount but it is later on, after your investment has increased in value and the dollar hasn't. Believe me, it helps you a lot more than it ever hurts. A good CPA will use it to make you money now. (Note: A 1031 tax deferred exchange can delay repayment of capital gains indefinitely.)

Here's how to play a decent game of real estate investment! Buy something at 20 percent or more below its market value. This is not hard to do. It may take you, as a new investor, three to six months to find it. You're learning curve will let you acquire under market value property at faster and faster rates from months to weeks to days. It takes practice. This book helps you move faster.

So you find a $100,000 property and you put down 20 percent (investor rate) as the down payment plus $2,500 in closing costs. The bank loans you $80,000 to buy it. If you're getting older, then pay someone to clean it and paint it. Get the bank to reappraise it for its true value of $120,000 or more. Take out an equity line and get all your money back, tax-free. Now let the tenants pay it off for you while it goes up in value and throws off positive cash flow, and shelters itself from taxation. This is not hard to do—this book is walking you through it.

I personally believe the hardest thing to do is to hold on to the real estate investments that you do acquire. What people tend to do is get tired or itchy, and they sell the goose. When you sell, you do get a lump sum of cash but now you have to go out and find more. This can become a revolving door. You have to keep going in and out of the market buying and selling again and again. Sound familiar?

If you just buy and don't sell your investments they will grow in value through inflation, appreciation, and equity accrual/mortgage reduction. Eventually, you will own them free and clear, and with four or five houses throwing off $1,000 or more each month, you will have approximately $60,000 a year in retirement income. I know my parents could live on that today. How about you?

Then as you get older, sell one—preferably the one you have spent two of the last five years in as your primary residence. The reason for this is because Uncle Sam says you don't have to pay any capital gains on the sale of your primary residence until you have exceeded $500,000 (for married couples) or $250,000 (for singles) in sheltered gains.

For example, let's say you just sell one home. You're in your early sixties and you have had the house for 25 years. Let's assume you paid $100,000 for it, and it has appreciated at a moderate rate of 5 percent each year on average. For those 25 years, its present value now would be $338,635.31. That is a capital gain of $238,635.31. You pay zero, *nothing*, in taxes on your profit, using your exemption up to a $500,000 lifetime cap for married couples or $250,000 for single folks.

The entire $338,635.31 is yours to do with whatever you please. It is 25 years later, so your buying power as a result of 3 percent inflation has eroded your ability to buy these same assets at such low prices. But you don't need more houses. You will use those assets (your houses) to pay for other things, such as living expenses, medical care, vacations, cars, and so forth—without having to work. Now think about all the people who have no real estate to fall back on. Ouch! That's no way to live.

No surprises here. You can actively manage your own properties for years and if you do it right and use my methods of acquiring tenants, you just might get lucky and get a lifetime tenant. I'm not going to let you say that it's impossible because I'm going to agree with you that it's probably not going to happen.

Here's what the statistics say (no charts or graphs). People move on average every five years so you should reasonably expect to have at least five different sets of tenants. That's fine because every five years, you can update your property's appearance and raise the rent to match current market conditions. Long-term tenants always seem to keep you from achieving a true market rent if they stay for 10 or 15 years, and they do stay. I see it all the time and I still get market rent.

The statistic that says people on average move every five years applies to you too. If you get itchy to move, don't sell. Just use equity lines to acquire your next, nicer house and don't move farther than 10 miles away from your investments. Even the pros blow it on this one.

If you pay attention to what I just said, you should retire comfortably, with more money than the average person ever needs. You have a choice.

I will use a true story to illustrate my point. My wife's uncle bought 2½ acres, in what his buddies from his telephone company job used to say was no man's land. He bought it for $15,000 in 1972. He financed his three-bedroom, two-and-a-half bath, two-car garage ranch style block construction home for an additional $32,000, for a total of $47,000.

He sold that house in 2001 using the methods discussed in this book for $365,000. He paid no commission and he paid no capital gains. That's a real life story of a $318,000 tax-free gain or profit on a $47,000 investment. He held onto it for 29 years, but now he has no money worries and lives a life of ease and comfort.

So my point: Collect a few houses and don't sell them. Rental real estate is a rewarding investment. It's not just the money; it's the value you personally deliver. I choose to live with purpose, passion, and desire. I can't do that in the stock market. That is the Magic Bullet of this chapter!

● ● ● ● CAPTURED IDEAS ● ● ● ●

Notes—*insights, ideas, actions to take*

_____

_____

_____

_____

_____

_____

Strategy—*planning for success*

_____

_____

_____

_____

_____

Tactics—*ways to achieve success*

_____

_____

_____

_____

_____

_____

Part III

Appendices

Proficiently Managing Affairs

To develop positive PMA, you must become *proficient at managing your affairs*. You need conscious competence. You must feel and believe and you also must achieve to a fair degree what you set out to do. If you are always confused, frustrated, or failing, then you cannot realistically maintain a positive mental attitude.

Many will read books and listen to tapes on developing PMA; however, if you're not gaining any proficiency on the real area you intend to succeed in, reading and listening to hype will become an elusive thief of your time. The result will likely be analysis paralysis. Because of the lack of relevant information being given, you will be no further along in your quest for understanding.

So what is my point? If you have no knowledge, no understanding, no ability, no clue, no experience, no help, no information, no idea of how to get started on achieving a successful or planned for outcome, your PMA is headed for the dumpster.

In order to develop your PMA, you must feel as though you can actually succeed in and at what you are all excited about. This said, the way to achieve PMA in real estate is to begin studying and applying basic proven methods that allow you to understand and duplicate a satisfactory result that, in turn, builds your confidence and competence levels in a direct way.

166 ● Magic Bullets in Real Estate

Upon each new level of understanding and achievement, your mental attitude improves. Things begin to make sense and you lean into more challenging arenas. It's a constant and gradual process. No hypnotist is going to make you a real estate wizard overnight. It takes practice, reading, application of the basics, repetition, and varying degrees of success and failure in your field of work.

The best teachers are those who have been where you want to go. Don't reinvent the wheel! Learn the basics, get feedback, and avoid the potholes and quagmires that sap you of the positive outcomes you seek.

I hope this book gives you the foundation to build and maintain your PMA properly. It's direct, proven, and easy to understand and apply. It covers many areas and creates clarity.

People waste years reading, listening, and doing the wrong stuff. They are sold a bill of goods by people who want their money or by misguided friends, relatives, and acquaintances who have supposedly found a better way. Every now and then, if you are lucky, you find a book that really does move you to action. Those are priceless works because they can change your life.

How do you know what to choose? Who to believe? What to read? Usually *you* have to decide on what you've read and what you've heard or seen. You also have your own ideas, which may or may not lead to a positive outcome. My advice to you is this: Look for people who offer you direct hard-hitting information that you can understand and use immediately to achieve your objective. Put the information to the test quickly. If it works, then do more of what they say to do. Exhaust the resource and get more of it. Keep doing that!

If it does not work, then return it for a full, no questions asked refund. Here's a key for you. When people offer you your money back or more, then they themselves believe in what they are telling you. They would go broke if it was fluff, hype, or useless information. So buy from people who assume all the risk up front for you.

Repeat the following to yourself:

I maintain my own PMA by doing the following things: I encourage others to talk about themselves and what they treasure most. I recognize their importance, respect their good judgment, and avoid arguments. If I am wrong, I admit it. I seek out people who excel at what they do and let them do the talking. I then get their point of view. I treat them with respect, dignity, honesty, and truthfulness—tenants included.

I challenge others to leave their comfort zones by making difficulties easy to conquer. Through praise and inspiration, I consider other people's strong points. I value their time and show interest in them, and I remember their names.

I try to be sympathetic, tolerant, and kind. I appreciate others but I do not flatter. Flattery is from the teeth, but appreciation is from the heart! I learn from everyone in some way.

I try to think of others more than myself, without having ulterior motives. I do things that require time, energy, unselfishness, and thoughtfulness. I listen and say thank you, and become the wiser for it.

In business, I try to be professional and follow procedures. I keep people informed and avoid procrastination. I delegate and maintain orderly forms, desks, files, and applications. I try to absorb criticism constructively and express appreciation for other people's time. I focus on self-reliance, initiative, and self-control, and concentrate on improving my reasoning abilities.

Use willpower, ambition, persistence, and memory to act with definite purpose and try to pass it on to those around you.

I recognize human dynamics such as the handshake, tone of voice, posture, and carriage of the body. I pick up vibrations of thought and pay attention to body adornment.

Others see me for who I am. How I think determines that. I dress well and it makes me look and feel sharp. I get quality clothes, food, friends, and information, and I think of myself as sharp, clean, together, intelligent, informed, and interesting. I practice uplifting praise and self-improvement in academics, and with family and friends. I run negative, time-wasting dream thieves out of my life.

I recognize the following time thieves: lack of motivation, mistakes I make because of my own failure to listen, indecision, poor planning, lack of discipline, unclear goals, conflicting priorities, poor delegation or communication, no procedure, equipment failure, interruptions, meetings, poor estimates, junk mail, red tape, oversleeping, low morale, and negative attitudes.

I build self-confidence through preparation. I take action that cures fear. I identify, admit, accept, and deal with fear accordingly, using words like *can, possible, will, want, do, today, goal,* and *love.* I eliminate words like *can't, impossible, won't, worry, someday, difficult, problem,* and *hate.*

I force myself to act confidently. I sit up front, make eye contact, walk faster than most, speak up when I have something to say, and wear a smile quite often. I try to radiate confidence, making sure I am tactful, mature, courteous, and decisive.

I try to think creatively. I believe there are new ways of doing things. I am receptive to and welcome fresh ideas. I soak them up. I ask, "How can I do this better?" Encourage others to talk, test new methods, listen, concentrate, and emulate. Ask intelligent people questions, write ideas down, and mix with people of different occupational backgrounds.

To stay informed about real estate, I read classifieds and sales magazines, and select good articles. I read books, talk to other real estate investors, and observe local trends and conditions in the marketplace. Circulate to percolate!

I try to know what people want: good health, happy and healthy children, money and the things it will buy, the feeling of being important and appreciated, and sexual gratification.

● These are positive emotions—desire, faith, love, enthusiasm, romance, and hope.

● These are negative emotions—fear, jealousy, hatred, revenge, greed, and anger.

● These are feared most—poverty, criticism, poor health, loss of someone, old age, death, and public speaking.

Knowing what people want, how they feel, and what they fear helps me to help them more.

If you get mad at people, then at least be angry with the right person to the right degree at the right time for the right purpose in the right way. Personally, I prefer to forgive and forget…it's easier! And people appreciate me more for being the saint that I'm not.

How does one succeed using all this positive mumbo jumbo? It's simple! Get your PMA and go to work using your knowledge and excellence, and give yourself to others.

● Life by Design

What is it that you want? How badly do you want it? Why do you want it? How do you intend to get it? What will you do if you get it? Who will help you? What will you sacrifice to get it? How long will it take?

Questions, questions, questions! They all need to be answered by you. Don't worry. I'm going to help you answer these questions before you finish this book. The beginning of this exercise is an introduction to how a goal begins to formulate in your subconscious before your consciousness defines it.

The very word "goal" signifies achievement, a desirable sought-after end result. Unlike a hockey game, your personal goals are not one-shot deals. You don't win or lose in one night. It takes a lifetime—and in life, you can't lose until you're dead!

So fear not, brave souls; your objective will be to try everything along the way that will not work until you find the one thing that does. It is a fact: It is impossible to succeed without failing.

Why do I say this? Am I trying to discourage you? No, not at all. I am simply trying to set the stage. This is serious business and if you don't have the guts and fortitude, you won't follow through. Only 1 in 20 people does—that's 5 percent of the total population and they alone control half of this world's wealth.

You are responsible for making your dreams reality, and the starting point is to bring those dreams to life by writing them down. No matter how many perceived failures or injustices you have received in your lifetime, if you look at them as stepping stones to success, you are one step closer to your goal. You weren't dealt a bad hand; in fact, you were given about a one in eight million shot at being conceived and given a life in the first place. Congratulations! You were the strongest swimmer before you were ever born.

Instead of telling you how important goals are, I'm going to show you. Then maybe you will understand how exactly it is they do work. Before we are through, you should be able to have a goal outlined that will help you define and narrow your focus into a usable format for success. I want you to relax and enjoy my story. It will show you the first step that is required to begin the goal outline. After the story, we will finish up the process and you will have a real estate goal.

Let me begin by saying that a goal needs to be very specific and defined so that you can really focus on those things that will help you get the job done. That's not saying it has to be complicated, but it needs to be focused. For example, if your goal is to get to heaven, then turn right and go straight!

The trouble with most of us is clearly defining what we want so we can follow a plan to a foreseen conclusion. There will be obstacles and roadblocks, setbacks and disappointments, with even the best-laid plans, so you really need a deep conviction to pursue your talent in an almost obsessive manner.

Here is my story: I was born Thomas Daniel Auito on July 30, 1963, in Detroit, Michigan. My last name means "help" in Italian. This has *helped* me from the time I realized that I was born to help. Given names are often an indication of your forefather's trades and traits. For example, the "Smiths" may have been blacksmiths or tradesmen in earlier times.

Now it's not enough to just know your roots but also to recognize your talents and abilities. These will be your areas of excellence, and in all probability, they will give you your best shot at success. In my case, a natural force drives me to help other people and I have had to develop people skills and a genuine interest in others to fully understand how I could help them.

I was 26 years old before I discovered my passion was real estate. What a great way to help people. After all, what is the most important and costly investment of a person's life? Of course, I am referring only to the financial spoke in the balanced wheel of life.

We are looking for your major purpose, a lasting contribution, your gift to all mankind. You must be satisfied with yourself before you can ever help those around you. It is to some degree selfish, but you must have a feeling of self-worth before PMA can be developed.

Back to the story: At the age of 26, I realized that real estate was what "turned me on." It was like a light switch that had only one position—*on!*

I was ignited. The burning desire had been lit. For the past 14 years, I have been obsessively driven on autopilot to devour all the knowledge I can grasp regarding real estate. Believe me when I say, not a day goes by that I don't help someone to live better and feel better by explaining to them how real estate can work for them in whatever capacity they need.

As a result of a passion for real estate and people, I am constantly driven to learn more, do more, be more, and help more than any nine-to-five job could ever demand of me. I dream about it and come up with more and more solutions to my demand to succeed at helping other people; it truly is an obsession.

My wife thinks I'm nuts but she understands, so I have her support. That is an extremely important point. You need support from your loved ones to truly be in harmony with your chosen passion. That also brings up the point that all seasoned goal setters will *show* people as opposed to *tell* people about their goals. Eighty percent of the population is negative—don't let them throw water on your flame!

This book is a way for me to potentially help millions of people all at once. I consider it my gift to mankind, so to speak, because it's my special talent and laser-focused attempt at giving all of what I have to give for a pittance to everyone who finds it. I just want to scream out to the world that here lies an answer to a few of life's questions. Please pass it on!

Now after reading my story, you may begin to realize that your true talent, gift, desire, passion, or ability lies somewhere else! Maybe in art, athletics, auto repair—it really doesn't matter. The same principles apply and if you can become so focused on whatever it is that drives you, then the forces of nature will propel you to achieve your destiny. It's a law of nature—you'll either succeed or die trying. But you will be living your dream until the end.

Here are the steps to success:

1. Ask yourself, "What do I really want?"
2. Believe you can have it.
3. Write it down.
4. What benefits will achieving the goal provide?
5. What do I need to help me succeed?
6. When do I want to attain my goal?
7. What, if anything, is holding me back?
8. What additional information do I need to help me succeed?
9. Who can help me?
10. Be specific and write the plan.
11. Visualize it as if it has already happened.
12. Decide now to *never quit* and persist until you succeed.

You may review the entire outline that follows, before you answer the first question to spark your desire. Throughout this outline, add notes and further details; be as specific as you can.

Regarding life goals, think about your most intense, burning desire. Write it as clearly and vividly as possible, focusing on the things you want and writing them as if they have already happened. You will want to come to a definite realization of why your desire is so strong. Look deep within to define your motivation for following this path. Use the lines that follow.

_____

_____

_____

_____

_____

_____

_____

_____

_____

_____

_____

_____

● Your Decision Process Guide

Throughout this exercise I urge you to make notes, highlight, underline, and further refine and define the items that are of interest to you. Write in the margins, after sentences, and in the spaces provided. The more thoughts you capture, and the more possibilities and insights you can recognize, the better your outcome. You are about to enter an insight-filled idea field. It is designed to help you focus on those things that will get you organized in a manner that will allow you to follow a plan geared to your own abilities, wants, needs, and desires. When you are finished, the only thing that will stop you from taking the needed action to succeed is you! You will have a plan that will work *if* you work it. No one can or will do this for you; it is entirely up to you! If you have read the entire book, then you are ready to take the final step and put it all into action. I absolutely believe this, and so should you. Let go of your fear and come with me *now!*

Underline what interests you most: condominiums, vacation/resort property, single-family homes, duplex, triplex, fourplex, apartments (five or more units), hotels/motels, strip malls, office complexes/small professional buildings, mobile home parks/individual trailers, storage units/yards, parking lots, garages, restaurants, lounges, stores, factories, refineries, farms, raw land, theaters, sports complexes.

In the space below, detail what type of real estate you have chosen to pursue, where it is located, and who will use it.

_____

_____

_____

_____

_____

Explain it in detail

_____

_____

_____

_____

_____

_____

_____

Underline what you are good at or feel you would enjoy; also circle the activities you dislike or feel you are not suited for:

A. Talking to buyers, sellers, and renters; goal-setting tracking and monitoring; analyzing numbers; researching public records; negotiating with lenders; performing property repairs; calculating returns; bookkeeping; financing deals; preparing and filling out legal documents.

B. Looking at many properties; decorating and painting; evaluating potential uses; making cold calls to sellers; structuring creative deals; making offers; managing tenants; selecting and directing contractors; finding alternative lenders, money, and partners.

Those who choose more items in A, tend to be left-brained (i.e., logical, verbal, mathematical, rigid, stoic). Those who choose more items in B, tend to be right-brained (i.e., images, feelings, pictures, creative, flexible, emotional).

What does the above reveal about your personality? Are you left- or right-brained? You actually are both, but one side is typically more dominant than the other.

Use the following checklists to define your goal. Be specific and detail exactly what it is you want to do and why.

Here is an example of a goal statement:

> I want to buy a fixer upper in the Jones Creek area for 30 percent or more below market price. I want something that needs minor repairs and a cosmetic makeover. I will rehab it after work and on weekends, then sell this property at full market price *by owner* using the methods learned in *Magic Bullets in Real Estate* and net a $10,000 profit within three months.

My goal in real estate is to:

● Buy my own home without paying a sales commission to a real estate broker or agent.

● Sell my own home without paying a sales commission to a real estate broker or agent.

● Rent my own home out to others, paying no management fees.

● Build my own home or homes for others.
● Buy and sell for quick profits.
● Buy, repair, rent, and hold.
● Buy to create a positive monthly cash flow of x amount per month.
● Buy to lease for the long term.
● Buy to lease with options to buy given to others.
● Buy substantially below market value by at least 20 percent.
● Buy with nothing down, using none of my own money.
● Buy and/or sell by owner paying no commissions.
● Buy to subdivide, develop, or change use.
● Buy for speculation or appreciation value in growth areas.
● Buy as tax shelter, inflation hedge, or long-term investment.
● Buy foreclosures, probate, or tax sale properties.
● Lend money to others for fixed returns or percentage cuts.
● Be a limited partner in real estate ventures.
● Invest in tax lien certificates or real estate investment trusts.
● Become a full time investor or real estate broker.
● Other: Be specific.

_____

_____

_____

_____

_____

_____

Indicate your start date for achieving your goals:
_____ (hint: today's date). Then, use the checklist below to describe your motivation.
● What benefits will I receive by achieving my goal?
● A flexible work schedule.
● More time with family.

- More security.
- More money.
- Freedom to choose how much I want to work and make.
- A variable work environment.
- Higher self-esteem and satisfaction.
- Greater opportunity to help others.
- A business of my own, doing what I love.
- Pay fewer taxes, shelter gains, and beat inflation.
- An opportunity to learn and use new skills.
- Pride of ownership.
- Increased savings.
- Direct control of investment portfolio.
- The use of leverage to increase wealth.
- Other: Be specific as to how the benefit will work to accomplish the feeling of achievement.

For example:

I will have a greater satisfaction as a result of providing a quality home to someone else who is not in a position to live in a home of their own at this time. I will also offset my expenses and regular income by taking deductions and using depreciation to shelter gains. Moreover, I will set up equity lines of credit to allow for more flexibility, security, and opportunity in the future.

Start date when I will commit to doing some or all of the following things: _____.

● What am I willing to *give* in return for these benefits?
● I will devote one half hour each day to study real estate investment.
● I will create a budget and begin to pay off any credit card debt within two weeks.
● I will attend a real estate seminar or event within one month.
● I will ask a real estate professional to be my mentor within five weeks.
● I will get preapproved for a loan within two months.
● I will inspect five properties a week until I buy one within three months.
● I will review real estate classifieds daily for applicable information.
● I will make at least two real estate–related calls per day.
● I will review my real estate goals at least twice daily.
● I will seek out and interview other real estate–minded investors.

For example:

I will read for 30 minutes between 8:30 and 9:00 P.M., Monday through Friday. I will add $50 extra to my Visa payment starting with the next bill. I will drive through the Jones Creek area on my way home from work on Tuesday and Thursday of next week. I will start a subscription to my local newspaper and focus my attention on reading ads that are of interest to me concerning my real estate investment program guidelines.

_____

_____

_____

_____

_____

_____

What do I *need* to help me achieve my goals?

- Support of those closest to me.
- A positive attitude of belief with a clear vision.
- A strong will and desire to persist through adversity.
- A completed loan application to determine assets and liabilities.
- A current credit report to see and correct blemishes.
- More knowledge of financing methods and alternatives.
- An initial set of books to structure my investments plan of attack.
- A mentor and other professionals who have the knowledge and contacts I need.
- An appraisal course to help me to better understand value and markets.
- A reliable car, cell phone, and professional clothing to project the right image.
- Copies of offer sheets, sales contracts, lease agreements and inspection guides for review and understanding of the finer points.
- A specific written goal plan to refer to twice daily for progress measurement.
- Other:

_____

_____

_____

_____

What definite deadlines and dollar values do I want to set?
I will:

- Set 30-,60-, and 90-day short-term goals.
- Set 6-, 9-, and 12-month medium-range goals.
- Set two-, three-, and five-year long-range goals.
- Reset new deadlines if initial goals are overly optimistic.

● Set a date to go to the bookstore to purchase reference materials.

I want:

● To make $10,000 profit on my first deal by _____.
● To have two rental properties valued at $235,000 by _____.
● To have 10 properties valued at $1,175,000 by _____.

I will be more specific and detail exactly how and when I will achieve the goals I have set.

_____

_____

_____

_____

_____

_____

_____

_____

_____

What is the *biggest* obstacle that is stopping me from starting today?

● My spouse or partner doesn't want me to do this.
● I don't know where to start.
● Procrastination—the I-will-do-it-tomorrow syndrome.
● I don't have any money or resources.
● I don't understand how to buy with nothing down techniques.

● There is too much competition right now.
● I can't find any good deals. I don't know where to look.
● I am afraid to try. I may lose money. I lack confidence.
● Other people keep telling me it won't work.
● I can't stand rejection or dealing with other people.
● It's a buyer's or seller's market. The timing's not right.
● I'm too busy, stressed out, tired, weak, uneducated, poor, lazy, scared, or sick. (To this, I say, baloney! You are perfectly capable. Remember, action cures fear. Do something!)
● Other:

_____

_____

_____

_____

_____

What additional information do I need to achieve my goal? I need:
● More real-life examples of how others have succeeded.
● To go to a homebuyer's seminar to understand the basics.
● To study and practice real estate techniques and procedures.
● To ask investors, lawyers, title companies, bankers, real estate agents, and appraisers lots of questions to further clarify my understanding of _____.
● To read as much information as it takes to better understand.
● A general review of real estate math to properly figure profit and expenses.
● To learn how to make offers and negotiate better.
● To read the classifieds and call to ask sellers specific questions.

● To be more honest with myself and write my plans down.
● Other:

_____

_____

_____

_____

_____

Who can help me most right now, in order of importance?

● My spouse or significant other—to provide moral support.
● Close friends, relatives, and goal-oriented partners—financing.
● A mentor to provide instruction, forms, knowledge, ideas, and contacts.
● Network members, bankers, lawyers, real estate brokers and agents, appraisers, tradesmen.
● Joint business partner—for money, resources, references, contacts, shared load.
● Limited partner—50 percent split, one provides time and labor, other provides funds.
● A seasoned investor—your labor, their expertise.
● Good contractor/handyman to help calculate repair costs and also to do repairs.
● Other:

_____

_____

_____

_____

_____

What will I give in return to others for their help?

	HOW MUCH?	WHEN?	ON WHAT?
● Money			
● Time			
● Effort			
● Labor			
● Attention			
● Written promises			
● Collateral			
● Appreciation			
● Consideration			
● Respect			
● Guaranteed assurances			
● Proof of the ability to contribute time, labor, funds, and ideas			
● Services from regular job			
● Personal property			
● Promissory notes			
● Liens			
● Share or percentage of profits or property rights			
● Notarized agreements of compensation based on performance			
● Other:			

Be specific and write the plan by taking all the information you have underlined, highlighted, or written in, and detail what you want, when you want it, and where you are at now. List your obstacles, and the information and people you will need to overcome them according to your plan.

My plan, including obstacles, is as follows:

_____

_____

_____

_____

_____

_____

_____

_____

You have the details, now visualize an absolute clear picture in your mind using what you have written to create a vision as if your goal has already been achieved. Read this in the morning and just before bed. Believe that it is happening and it soon will!

Ultimate goal—

_____

_____

_____

_____

_____

_____

_____

_____

Never quit!

Appendix B

Case Studies and Examples

Let me tell you the story of Dan (His name really was Dan. I'm honest in this book!), a 21-year-old friend of mine, his wife, and their new baby. Dan wanted to buy a house, so I began the process of saving him years of trial by fire. I asked him what type of home he thought he would be comfortable with and the price range. He indicated a three-bedroom home for around $100,000 would be about right.

Knowing what he wanted and the area he wanted it in, I took him shopping. We hit the for-sale-by-owner homes—FSBOs—first, as I always do since I know they won't be trying to add the commission figure into their price. For instance, at 6 percent of $100,000 he will get $6,000 more "house" for his dollar.

We found a home that was priced below its true appraised value and had no commission being paid to a flat-fee company for its advertising effort. Here our seller did come down from his asking price of $103,000 to $99,000 with no commission to pay. As a result he had room to go lower without losing out. Just to update you, these same homes in the subdivision are now selling for $140,000 two years later—I just verified that. That is about a $35,000 profit after expenses if Dan sold today!

In addition to the FSBOs, I told him we would be looking at properties represented by discount companies that help distressed sellers further part with their money and property. Using a cheesy company to help sell property is penny-wise and pound-foolish. If you're going to use a professional, then get a real professional. (My definition of "cheesy company" is a company with poor name brand recognition, one or two local offices, and poor marketing exposure channels established. These companies charge a minimal flat fee to put up signs, take incoming calls to give details, and refer the negotiating parties to various service providers to effect the transaction. These are the worst. My point again is if you're going to use a real estate company then use professionals who offer full service from beginning to end.)

So off we go. After a day or so, we have found our house. Sure enough, El Cheeso, Inc., has a sign on it. The screen doors are flapping in the breeze and the weeds are dancing on the lawn, but this house has three bedrooms, two baths, and a one-car garage with a fenced yard. It's listed for $110,000. Well, because there is a divorce in progress, and a new girlfriend who doesn't like the place, and El Cheeso giving no representation, I negotiate for Dan and he gets it for $99,000. What's so great about this deal is the exact same floor plan was for sale in another house down the street for $25,000 more.

Note: There are some very capable discount brokerage firms offering great rates to handle transactions from start to finish at 2 percent commission rates. Just be sure they approach the sale of your home with all the professionalism of the larger market players. Times are changing and the Internet has brought more power to the FSBOs who want to assume some of the functions that traditionally could only be handled by agents. Interview prospective companies and by all means get their commitments to you in writing.

The moral of the story is good things come to those who deserve it, and that is another key to real estate. You must work hard so others will take notice of you and help you succeed.

Here's a beauty for you. This is about being in real estate circles and keeping your eyes and ears open—and often your "yapper" closed.

This is the story of Brian and Julie. Here we have two hardworking souls. They have been married for 20 years and they have weathered the storms of matrimony. Julie works at a real estate office as an office manager. No real estate license, but she works at an office that sells a lot of waterfront property. So we are talking about location and being in the right place at the right time, and here comes a seller in the door of the office stating she is going to sell her older waterfront home. She is willing to take $180,000.

Julie tells Brian, they look at it, and sure enough, this pearl is right on the water. She's a gem waiting to be polished up, so Brian and Julie sell their condominium and move in. Well, they aren't making any more waterfront property, so Brian goes to work polishing this jewel up.

Now, they have bought this house under market value in an appreciating market. So about one and a half years later, this property is worth over $350,000 and still climbing. Well, Brian is no dummy, so he gets to know his neighborhood. He strolls, takes walks and notices—you guessed it—a vacant, neglected jewel on an inside double lot. He tracks down the elderly lady, who is living with her sister, through the county records office and buys the house, including the extra lot, for a total of $120,000. Now Brian can walk to his new "jewel" and he starts polishing it. The neighbors start noticing and are amazed at his deal. He has offers of $180,000, $200,000—and $60,000 for just the lot. You name it. Now that the exposure is there, everyone wants a piece of it.

Well, this is what Brian did. He rented out his first house, moved into the second one, and used plans that I gave to him to build a third house on the vacant lot, using the equity he accumulated from the first house that went up so much. And here's how this thing shakes out: $180,000 for his first house and it's value goes up to $365,000; he picked up the next jewel for $120,000 and he paid cash using the equity from the first house. He took out a new mortgage on his second house for $120,000 and built a third. The value at last count was $815,000 and he owed a grand total of $300,000. That's a half-million-dollar profit in five years!

Now what does this story tell us? It says:

● Work hard.

● Keep your eyes open.

● Use equity lines.

● Don't sell.

● Learn how to be a landlord.

● Be in locations that appreciate.

● Buy things that have limited availability.

● Know how to research owners and repair property.

● Get your partner or spouse's help.

● Use knowledgeable friends to help you see potential.

Can you get any more lessons out of this story? I'm sure you can. Just read it again and think about it. Jot down your ideas and put them to work. Real estate is not that hard, folks. You can do it. With a few Magic Bullets, some spark plugs, and a good mentor to show you how, you can do it too!

● Log Home Story

The following story—about a log home—has a few good lessons and observations that no doubt can be used by you to take advantage of hidden opportunities that often lie in plain view. Most people, however, have not been trained to recognize them.

It begins with a classic log home package, engineered, manufactured, approved, and delivered for use in Alaska. A friend of mine built the home in 1996; I helped him pour the foundation. This leads to our first observation in analyzing this deal: If you *know the full history of a property*, your confidence and position on the deal can be enhanced.

You can begin to research history and succession of ownership through county records, tax rolls, and by contacting previous owners as far back as you possibly can. Optimally you want to end your search by getting to the original owner and builder of the property.

My friend—an intelligent perfectionist—built this house himself. This gave me the confidence of knowing that this owner-built home was a solid structure through and through, not to mention that when the energy rating, otherwise known as a "blow test," was conducted the house was so tight (no air leaks), he had to artificially ventilate it.

At this point, I had the following information: *I know who built it, the quality of construction, its energy rating, and its value,* based on what my friend had sold it for to the new owners. This brings us to our next phase of the investigation, the current owners.

Now we turn our attention to the current owners who are selling and the history behind them. Originally they paid $159,000, which by some strange coincidence was the asking price. (I'm sure if the asking price was $160,000, it would have appraised for that but my friend made it appear cheaper by keeping below the higher $160,000 bracket. This is known as a pricing strategy.)

Our research on the new owners revealed that they had been relocated from New Jersey and they had one child. The neighbor, who is a home inspector and general contractor, tells me a few more details about the family, their habits, and the upgrades, improvements, and modifications that have been made to the home. Once again I'm getting good signals that the home is a good one, but the owners are a little squirrelly as to their habits and design choices.

Here is where opportunity starts knocking, folks. When you have people who do things that are out of the mainstream of what most people do, you will notice that when it comes time to sell, many buyers are turned off by the nonconformity of the home's general appearance. Let me explain.

These people did the following things: first, they installed a spiral staircase and painted it a purplish-pink. Yuck! This alone was said to have turned off more than one potential buyer. Also, the original paint had pencil and marker lines scribbled here and there, the faucets and caulking needed some repair, the glass in one of the kitchen cabinets was missing, the walls needed new paint, and the yard was overgrown. Along with a few other small details, this was all cosmetic, but people couldn't look past it.

Let's get to the real "nails in this coffin" of lost resale value. The following information deals with choosing a good real estate agent who will properly handle your affairs—if, in fact, you cannot do them yourself, although you should actively participate. Here is where this agent's ineptitude will seal these relocated owners' fate. Let's set the stage: We are now at 2003; our sellers are being transferred and are moving after five years. This is right in keeping with the national average, which says that people tend to move every five years. So in conjunction with the move, a relocation company becomes involved. Here comes the red tape!

Our sellers chose a local real estate agent who works half days and delivers newspapers the other half (not too professional). The agent does nothing to prepare the home to show well and—the topper on this one—was the fact that the agent had left an inflatable monstrosity of what used to be a swimming pool/fun center half-deflated with stagnant water, breeding mosquitoes at the base of the entryway stairs. What a first impression and such an easy fix!

That's just the beginning because now our agent by some stroke of luck has found someone willing to pay $156,000 for this eyesore, but the agent doesn't research anything and can't come up with the proper documentation for the original well and septic approval. Therefore, the relocation company sends out its own engineer to backtrack, and he blows the deal clear out of the water because he doesn't know local protocol and has no original paperwork either. As a result the potential buyers back out and the house sits empty for another six months. Meanwhile, our poor relocated owners back in New Jersey are still paying a mortgage on this while facing percolation tests for a special $10,000 septic tank that isn't needed.

What we have now is a classic stigmatized home and its value is plummeting. The costs are rising and the agent is plumb worn out from phone calls, septic tank manufacturers, engineers, state regulators, cancelled contracts, and the sellers' constant groaning. Things are looking pretty bleak.

Enter the white knight—the educated investor. What a relief! Someone who knows what to do! Upon watching this carnival of events unfold for a while, I decided to step in. What finally drove me to act was a call to my office that presented an endgame. What I mean by this is a military officer called to ask if I had a place he could rent for two years. At that moment, I told him I might and I would get back to him.

The first thing I had to do was to inspect the property; repairs were mostly cosmetic. Next, I went and drilled the agent for information and at this point, the agent was giving me every scrap of insider information that could legally be disclosed. I now knew this property could be had for $137,000. Additionally, I would get a 3.5 percent commission and the seller would pay the closing costs! I had a solid two-year tenant lined up, willing to pay $1,350 a month and his own utilities. An appraisal had been done six months earlier on the deal that had fallen through and it pegged the value at $160,000.

The only thing left to do was to get the original documentation from the owner-builder that would resolve the septic issue. I called him up—he lived less than a mile from his old log home—and he said, "Sure, Dan, I have all the paperwork right here…the current agent never asked me for it!" I looked it over and here is what he had: the original design and construction survey, the engineer's original approval of well and septic, the building department's approval, and the department of environmental conservation's waiver granting permission to install according to the plans. This completely removed all obstacles to financing and the appraiser agreed. Problem solved in less than two hours!

The green light was flashing, so I had the lieutenant sign a two-year lease, give me a check for one and a half month's rent up front, plus last month and a half month as a security deposit for a total of $4,050. I then bought the house! I painted, cleaned, trimmed, and tweaked the house. In eight days it became a beautiful showplace on 1.77 acres worth $27,000 more than I paid for it less than a month before. In addition, there is a positive cash flow of more than $300 a month above my mortgage and escrow payment obligation. I would also like to add that the spiral staircase is now painted white and stands as the most beautiful centerpiece to a home that anyone could ask for! All it needed was a vision, some labor, and paint.

Let's hit the high points and drive home some of the lessons from this series of events:

● Research and obtain as much history on the property as you can.

● Pay attention to the quality of construction and types of materials used.

● Use comparable sales, costs of construction, recent sales prices, assessments, and existing appraisals, and take into account the cost to cure existing defects to begin to determine a reasonable value.

● Look for easily correctable problems that turn other people off and correct them.

● Pay attention to landscaping and the ability to improve upon its appearance.

● Analyze the series of events that led up to the sale and the seller's current position.

● Have a plan or endgame in mind for using the property once you acquire it.

● Always try to ask less than full asking price and be prepared to walk away if you don't get the price and terms you feel justify the purchase.

● Stay abreast of market conditions and events and be patient; these deals will come your way when you are prepared to see them.

Have you ever been really good at something and been able to step back and see the whole thing for what it was? You just know exactly how to do it and you can see the end result clearly in your mind before you start? It's predictable to you. It's almost second nature, so you are comfortable doing it. Your comfort zone is such that you can do it in your sleep.

I've gotten that way with certain types of real estate, and I see people every day who are so afraid of taking the first step they are literally paralyzed. They make excuses and put it off, rationalize, and live a quiet life of desperation. They don't trust themselves, and as a result of the unknown, they can't trust anyone else either. This is a vicious cycle because the longer they wait, the more it reinforces their beliefs.

I just want to grab them by the collar, take them to the bank, and make them tell the banker, "Prequalify me!" Then I'd like to walk them out the door and show them how to do something that will change their life forever, and that is to buy the first property, then a second. Their fear will be gone and they will soon be of service to everyone who is ready for their assistance.

Let me say this: After you finish reading this book, your fears will be subdued , you will do something, and your life will change. If you cannot succeed with what I am intent on showing you, then something is not right. I believe your lack of desire would be your major obstacle, so if that's the case, read *Think and Grow Rich* by Napoleon Hill and come back to me then. (Download it for free at www.magicbullets.com.)

● Mobile Home Park

Let's get on with another story. This one is about a family that had business interests outside of real estate investing and as a result of the successes of their other businesses they had fairly large sums of money to play real estate like a monopoly game. Power can be dangerous in the wrong hands!

This flush-with-cash family saw an opportunity to take advantage of an overlooked or left alone market. That market is the old-fashioned trailer park, or shall we say mobile home park.

Anyway, the way most mobile home parks came into existence was this: Usually a man of integrity and strong work ethic coupled with a love for his fellow man would buy a piece of land suitable to the placement of mobile homes. As people moved in, he and his wife would welcome them and the community would become established.

The private owner would dig his own sewer lines, cut his own roads, and landscape the park. Maybe he would put in the clubhouse complete with a swimming pool, shuffleboard, pool table, and meeting hall. As time marched on, the residents bonded with each other and a family-friendly community took root. Well, this man of integrity had a problem. Since all of his tenants were his friends, he was pressured not to raise the lot rents with inflation.

So the rents over the years were kept very low in the park and now this man and his wife are getting old. Perfect timing for our investors to come knocking and offer our private aging park owner a $2 million price for his 10 acres of mobile home lots. This is a once-in-a-lifetime offer and many park owners cashed out.

What people didn't see was these investors were systematically and methodically doing this all over the place and once they cashed out as many mom and pops as they could, they lowered the boom.

Now they—the investors—had control of many parks in the same areas and they started raising the lot rents. They didn't have any emotional ties to the residents, so it was a straightforward business deal: Pay the new higher rent or move.

The residents said, "To hell with you, new owner, we are moving." The residents started calling around to find another park with low rents but guess who owned those? Yep, our investors did, and those lot rents were going up too. So the mom and pops who didn't sell were full and it would cost on average about $7,000 to relocate to another park even if they could find a vacancy.

The old folks who had it so good for so long were faced with a new reality and that was that they had no choice but to pay up or move, and moving, in many cases, wasn't an option. These investors exploited a complete segment of the market and made millions and millions in profit and continue to do so today.

It wasn't long after this happened that you started seeing signs saying, "This is a resident-owned community." People eventually got smart and started buying that little lot that their trailer was sitting on and they began paying association dues for the clubhouse and security and grounds maintenance and road repair. The good ole days are nothing but a fond memory.

Life goes on, but America did not change for the better as a result of these types of people. Their only purpose was to make money; I believe they will die alone and in misery as a result of their way of life.

So, I ask you again, can you be passionate and put your heart into investing in real estate by investing the way our corporate investors did? I think not. Money is no good when you get it by deceitful ways. I encourage you to work at balancing your objectives. Lease optioning, flippers—you may be walking a fine line.

● Communal Living

Here's a flip side to communal living. This story is a happier scenario, so let's have a little joy here. I once lived in Key West and I lived off base. Well, I thought I lived next door to Noah, and it sounded as though he was building another ark. All summer long, hammers and saws seemed to be making some type of racket, so naturally being the neighbor I was, I got to know the man next door. He never went to work and I asked him one day, "Don't you have a job?" He kind of grinned, put his hammer down, and told me his story.

Mark and his brother were from the Northeast. They had a 30-room boarding house for college kids there, at something like $300 a month. That was about $9,000 a month. Mark would spend his time with his family in the Keys for the nine months that school was in session. His brother was a local up north and he took care of the toilets, faucets, doors, and windows. Yes, they had their very own "animal house" going on there, but Mark factored in the abuse and would spend two or three months a year putting the animal house back together while the animals went home for summer break.

Mark only worked three months a year and the house (ark) he built next to us was a masterpiece; it was beautiful. He was a master craftsman and he loved his work and spent a lot of his time with his family in a wonderful climate. Makes you kind of jealous, doesn't it? Well, don't let it because you can do it, too, but you must get started. Mark was 45 when I met him. I believe he was 25 when he got started, so my advice to you is to get started now!

Getting Started in Your Twenties

"How would you like to collect that rent as opposed to pay it!"

Naturally this question gets the attention of every young person, and with it, we can begin to open the door of enlightenment. I like to use the duplex example to illustrate the two homes under one roof concept. Some people are unfamiliar with what exactly a duplex is and how it works, so I simply state that quite often you find duplexes composed of one building that has two bedrooms and one bath on each side, all under one roof.

These are as easy to finance as a single-family home and in many cases allow you to qualify for a larger loan amount, which leads to using leverage and more of other people's money to get ahead faster in life. Let's say you find a duplex for $150,000. With 6 percent interest, your principal and interest would be $899.33 a month. To calculate insurance costs, we use an average of $5 per $1,000 of home value. So $5 x $150 = $750 a year for insurance. We divide that by 12 months to get a figure of $62.50 a month for insurance. We also have annual taxes that are based on what the home is worth multiplied by a millage, or mill rate. Let's use a tax rate of $11 per $1,000 of the home's assessed value: $11 x 150 = $1,650 a year. Now divide that by 12 months to get a monthly tax of $137.50 and by adding principal, interest, taxes, and insurance (PITI), we get a total monthly mortgage payment of $1,099.33.

When you rent one side out for approximately $750 a month, you are left to pay only $349.33 out of your own pocket. It is very plausible that this amount is much lower than the amount of rent someone is paying to live under another's roof. How can the average twenty-something get started? The answer most often begins with, "By getting preapproved for a loan." Bring the following things to the bank loan officer to get started:

● W-2s

● Tax returns for the past two years

● Three months of bank statements

● A copy of your credit report (although the lender will also likely run its own)

● A filled-out loan application

● Copies of titles to good collateral (if any)

● Three references

● The name of the person willing to co-sign, if possible

With these initial documents the lender can begin to process your application for a loan. He or she will determine your assets and liabilities (net worth) as well as verify where you live now, your credit history, and a host of other information that begins to validate your existence and ability to borrow money now and in the future.

Once they've had a chance to review and verify your information they can preapprove you for a certain loan amount. Once you're approved, you can begin your search for a home of your own. Typically, as a first-time homebuyer you will find that there are programs that let you put as little as 3 to 5 percent down in order to buy a home that satisfies the lender's guidelines according to its value and conformity. On a $150,000 loan, the down payment can be anywhere from $4,500 to $7,500.

There are ways to lower these costs and a great place to start is by attending a first-time homebuyer's class. These classes introduce you to the basics. They give you further information on programs currently available that may offer you the opportunity to buy with nothing down! So with that said, the next step is to get to a free class and become familiar with the process. Often I recommend going to the class before going to see a lender so you don't appear so green and unprepared upon your initial introduction.

The next issue that arises is where you can get the money to get started. I usually ask about savings, whether parents or grandparents can help, if the prospective buyers can sell valuable possessions, take a second job, get grants, gifts, use trust funds, personal loans or cosigners. A combination of these alternatives with a complimentary loan program usually gets the ball rolling. Options and hard money lenders usually come later as alternative funding and acquisition sources, so I won't confuse anyone with those now.

The bottom line is this: If you want something bad enough there is always a way!

The nice thing about duplexes is that the lender will take into account the fact that 75 percent of the rental income from the other side of the property can be used to offset your qualifying ratios, so in this case they can use 75 percent of the rental's $750 income to reduce the amount you must earn to qualify for what appears to be an unaffordable loan. Seventy-five percent of $750 is $562.50. Subtracting that amount from the original mortgage payment of $1,099.33 leaves you with a payment of $536.83, which the bank says you must be able to repay every month out of your own pocket. You can do this!

Can you begin to see how with a little information, effort, and belief, you can actually own something and pay less than what you are currently paying in rent?

Let's continue on with the way things begin to unfold once you begin the journey. Starting with the day you close the deal and become the new owner you will see that you now have just created a passive income stream that gives you an extra $750 a month without you having to punch a clock or trade a certain amount of hours to earn the money. Your new asset works for you day in and day out, constantly generating income for you while you go and do other things. This is leveraging your time and money in a very beneficial way!

You also will notice that at the closing of your purchase, the old owners who sold you this property had to prorate or give you a share of the rents due and any security deposits the tenants had given to them. Add to that the likelihood that your first house payment won't come due until about a month and a half after you move in, and you find yourself with, lo and behold, *extra money*, probably for the first time in quite a while!

Let's calculate it using simple math. Assuming you close on the 15th of the month, you will have 45 days before your first payment comes due. You will be credited with 15 days of rent, you will receive all security deposits of the tenant, you will receive another month's rent on the first of the month from your tenant, and you yourself will have no rent or house payment of your own to make for another whole month. What does all that add up to? Let's break it down:

● Fifteen days of rent equals $375

● A half month's rent as a security deposit equals $375

● A full month's rent in another 15 days equals $750

● No payment to the bank for another 30 days and you're not paying rent to anyone any longer, so you keep whatever you normally would have had to give to someone else as rent that month (let's say that was $500)

● Another payment to you for $750 from your tenant as well as you having to make your first mortgage payment of $1,099.33 on the 1st of the month, which comes 45 days later

Side note: If you decided to rent your second bedroom to a roommate, he or she would pay $500 a month and half your utilities as well, thus you're basically living in and owning this property for free. Say goodbye to all those student loans as you divert all these freed-up funds to pay off loans instead of a landlord!

Adding these up, we get $375 + $375 + $750 + $750 + $500 not paid to your old landlord. That equals $2,750 you will now have as a result of your first month and a half of ownership. Subtract your mortgage payment of $1,099.33 and you are left with a reserve fund of $1,650.67 in your account. Take your parents out to a steak dinner and celebrate—you've earned it!

Let's review: You decided to buy your own home; you made the choice early to offset expenses by looking at a multiple income property; you went to the homebuyer's class; you went to see a lender and got preapproved for a loan; you saved or arranged to have the necessary amount required to buy; and you hunted, searched, and analyzed more than a few properties in order to find a good one that would satisfy your criteria.

Your next phase is to begin to realize that you are now responsible for the welfare of another family or person because of your willingness to become a landlord. Your tenants pay rent and expect you to take care of their housing needs. If you chose a good property by carefully looking at plumbing, heating and air-conditioning, electrical, foundation, structure, roof, location, and price, then you should be well positioned to be able to successfully manage these duties. Often, as the new owner, you will begin to make improvements to the property such as painting, installing new carpet, and doing some inexpensive landscaping and repairs. These are the things that add value to your property and keep your tenants happy—and they don't break the bank!

With $1,650.67 in your bank account, you're not exactly Donald Trump just yet, but you're getting there. Smart landlords establish six-month reserve accounts and/or contingency funds, which protect them in times of *vacancies* or when expensive unforeseen *repair bills* pop up in addition to regular planned-for maintenance items. What I'm saying is don't spend your reserves frivolously. In my case, a steak dinner is a tradition but the major portion of your funds should only be used to build, protect, and enhance your asset's ability to produce and sustain income generation.

By taking on responsibility in the housing market at such a young age, you will have some added benefits and opportunities coming to you. You will have overcome fear and lack of understanding by acquiring your first property. In addition, you have begun to offset expenses while saving more money; you are establishing excellent credit while building assets; and you're gaining tax advantages while getting management, home buying, and repair education at an early age. These are outstanding life skills you can use for the rest of your life

This type of initial home-buying strategy can and does lead to more opportunities to grow and achieve further benefits besides those already mentioned. Individuals who learn to accept responsibility early will by nature grow more mature throughout the process and in effect create for themselves a higher status in the minds of others by being looked upon as a current homeowner and landlord. Once established, you will become known for what you can do.

In addition, when you meet someone who may become your spouse in the future, you will be in a much better situation to move up to a nicer, single-family home. You can simply rent out both sides of your duplex.

Let's assume two years have gone by, and you have been living in and improving your duplex all along. Assuming you bought a decent property in a good neighborhood and inflation and appreciation has been adding value along with your improvements, your $150,000 duplex should command a new appraised value of $175,000. Let me explain how the value grows: 3 percent annual inflation multiplied by $150,000 equals $4,500 the first year. Let's also say that appreciation due to demand also adds 5 percent, so 5 percent x $150,000 = $7500. Now $150,000 + $7,500 + $4,500 = $162,000, which represents the new value for year one. The second year we do the same math on $162,000 and we get $12,960 for year two. Adding that to $162,000 equals $174,960. (Okay, I was off by $40.) Don't forget any improvements and that you may have bought it at a discount because the old owners where motivated and you might find its worth even more.

Now over those two years you have also been paying that old mortgage of $1,099.33 each month and the principal amount that you owe on your loan has been reduced by an additional $3,965.96, leaving you with a loan balance of $146,034.04. The difference between the new appraised value of $175,000 and the current amount of $146,034.04 you owe equals $28,965.96. This number represents the equity, or value, that you currently own in the home. Knowing this, it is entirely possible to apply for and receive a home equity line of credit up to the full value of the new appraisal! If you haven't gone overboard on buying cars, boats, and running up other revolving debt and your significant other or spouse-to-be has a job and good credit with manageable debt, then the bank is going to approve this line of owner-occupied credit.

Now what you have done is set up a line of credit that can be used to buy a $145,000 single-family home with a 20 percent down payment. This allows you to avoid paying private mortgage insurance, thereby creating a very affordable new mortgage on your new family residence.

Note: Do not confuse homeowner's insurance with private mortgage insurance. PMI protects the lender while homeowner's insurance protects you. When you put down 20 percent of value on a home's purchase in the form of a down payment, you are in effect protecting the lender from yourself because if they foreclosed on you for nonpayment, they could sell the home fast for less than full value and still be paid in full. Don't pay for private mortgage insurance if you can avoid it!

Let's not forget that as the value of your duplex has risen the rents should also be increasing along the same lines. Instead of $750, you should reasonably expect to get $800 per month, per side, which now delivers $1,600 a month to your bank account. Unfortunately, you still have to pay for 28 more years on the original loan amount, so you will make that good old $1,099.33 payment as usual. That leaves you with $500.67 leftover to pay that new equity line back with. Your new $29,000 equity line, which you used as a down payment on your new home, costs you $336.71 at 7 percent for 10 years. Now $500.36 minus $336.71 leaves you with $163.96 leftover to maintain a nice little reserve account for vacancies and maintenance/repairs. This is a good example of how to transition to a secure lifestyle while using your existing asset base to buy more.

Break the mold and look at multiple income property to start:

● Go to a first-time homebuyer class to get ready.

● Go to a lender prepared to qualify for an affordable loan amount.

● Focus your effort on learning how real estate works.

● Realize the sooner you start, the better off you will be.

● Offset expenses by renting to others.

● Manage tenants, deposits, and property responsibly.

● Plan for the future using assets and equity lines to start.

● Keep reading and learning how to do new things with real estate.

● Find mentors and use knowledgeable people to help you along the way.

Appendix D
Professional Investor's Plan

Strategy as defined here is the science of planning and directing exactly how you intend to maximize your profit potential through investing in real estate. Without a sound strategy and consistently executable tactics you may find that the result of your labors have only led you to frustration and a less-than-sought-after result.

Here I would like to make just a few suggestions that will hopefully save you from wasting years of hard effort only to learn in the end that had you invested using a better strategy, you would have realized more profit, happiness, satisfaction, control, and free time as a result. I'm not going to make you wait to find out the secret, so here is the crux of this technique: Find 'em, don't fix 'em! It sounds easy, doesn't it? Please continue reading to get the full flavor of this topic. There are a few steps to follow if you are to succeed in using this method and you will really need to understand before you go and do it. I need to stop here and take into consideration the new investor who doesn't have a war chest of greenbacks to get started with.

If you're starting out with a small amount of capital then you will most likely have to find 'em *and* fix 'em on the first one or two properties. By finding them and fixing them, then selling on your own, you will limit the amount of initial expense that you incur. Naturally you will keep more of the profit as a result.

The trouble with this technique is that you eat up valuable time that could be more profitably spent on finding more great deals!

If you spend your day painting a property, how much have you saved or earned? Let's say a painter at $30 an hour multiplied by eight hours equals $240 dollars a day. You, in effect, have given yourself a new job that pays $30 dollars an hour. Instead of painting, let's say you hire the painter so that you can go hunt down another bargain property with a $20,000 margin of profit. Let's also assume that it takes 100 hours of effort to find, fix, and sell this property; $20,000 divided by 100 hours equals a $200-per-hour rate of pay. Don't work for $30 when you can work for $200!

By doing the first property using your own time and labor, you may get the most of that $20,000 dollar profit when you sell, but it will generally take you an average of three months to do it, or 480 hours. That boils down to $41.66 an hour and you can't look for more great deals. What this *will* do is give you the capital to pay someone else to do the labor on the next one. Once you have your nest egg you can begin to pay up to $5,000 for the labor, which includes materials. Now you let the lower wage scales do the dirty work of cleaning, repairing, painting, and installing new fixtures and you no longer spend your more valuable time doing low-paying labor jobs, so now you can quite feasibly make $20,000 and spend $5,000 to do it. This leaves you with $15,000 profit divided by 100 hours, which equals $150 an hour or five times the pay of the painter! Don't be a laborer if you don't have to be.

I hope you see how it pays to find them rather than fix them. Granted you're going to have to learn this higher skill of finding and evaluating good deals; however, throughout this book I've given you at least 150 ways to find those deals, such as from bandit signs, newspaper ads, bird dogs, professional search services, and so forth. You have the ammunition to launch a campaign that will yield plenty of these deals.

Once you find what appears to be a motivated, distressed, or disinterested seller, your next skill set will be to evaluate the property to ensure that a profit will result if you do proceed. Here again, you're focusing on plumbing, electrical, foundation, structure, roof, and location, since the rest will generally be cosmetic repairs that can be done quickly and inexpensively in an effort to realize the true value without going *broke!*

Once you have some accurate figures concerning a probable sales price, the cost of materials, labor, marketing time, and transfer costs you can project your profit. Will it yield $20,000 or more in 90 days? It should! If not, then you may consider passing on the deal and continue the hunt for another property that does satisfy your strategic objectives. Side note here: Often when you walk away from deals like this, they end up coming back to you later when the sellers can't sell. You'll have an opportunity to lower your offer to an amount that will satisfy your objectives and it will usually be accepted at that time.

Now that you have found, evaluated, and acquired the property, you will have to make the repairs. Here is where you play Mr. or Ms. general contractor. By hiring licensed and bonded professionals who come highly recommended you begin to pass off the labor issues back to the lower earning wage scales so that you can get back to finding more good deals.

Note: One trick to getting good workers and companies is to ask appraisers who they would recommend for certain jobs if *they* needed work done. Appraisers know a lot about value, folks! They seldom steer you wrong. So build your network through their referrals.

Another way to save money is to begin getting familiar with local suppliers of all types of construction materials. I'm not talking truss members and cinder blocks but you will have to create your repair list—otherwise known as a punch list—often. You can create this list of items typically needed to do fixing and replacing in a few short hours. By using your notes from your initial evaluation, you'll be halfway home. These items may include tile, vinyl, carpet, or wood for floors, toilets, faucets, sinks, tubs, vanity cabinets, mirrors, towel bars, light switches, electrical receptacles, light kits, ceiling fans, knobs, handles, lock sets, and paint to make the property look and smell new again. Now you can spend another eight hours shopping for and scheduling the dates of delivery and installation for the larger items but that is where your labor ends and you revert back to the supervisory role of periodic inspections to insure the laborers and contractors are getting the job done on schedule.

Up to this point we have done four things: We have found, evaluated, acquired, and are repairing. With these steps behind you, the next step will be to start the marketing efforts to find a buyer for this beauty. By pricing it right and advertising it for sale to the entire market of potential buyers, the word will get out. You can help that word circulate by using newspapers, yard signs, corner signs, word of mouth, flyers, fact sheets, neighbor alerts, network partners, and a host of other avenues of approach that can almost guarantee you a steady stream of buyers when the time to sell is near.

So you have found, evaluated, acquired, repaired, and marketed the property. Now the final step is to get the sales contract signed and a closing date scheduled. This should all be accomplished in about 90 days and you will have cleared no less than $15,000 as a result. Your results may vary—it could be lower, and quite possibly higher depending on how good you are! I'm giving you the overview here. You will be doing many tasks along the way that are not being explained in depth here.

You *will* have capital gains taxes. However, when you keep every receipt and use a CPA to do your taxes, the process will be fairly painless. This work will pay very well regardless of that fact. By having two or three of these rehabs going on at any one time and just one closing a month, you should be making over $100,000 a year, after Uncle Sam gets his.

Many highly trained or experienced investors never even touch the property. They simply find great deals, handle some paperwork, and sell it for less than they could get if they spent more time on it. These people are leveraging their time and techniques to squeeze out the maximum profit in the shortest possible time with the least amount of effort. I don't condone being a paper pusher and taking advantage of other people's ignorance or misfortunes by doing paper trades. I personally have a hard time finding value in deeds done by using such methods. This is why I have given you a value-driven road map to follow in this brief report. I sincerely hope you will create value for those who depend on you to deliver in an honest and caring professional manner. Happy hunting!

Networks create stability and growth opportunity

You have the power to change thousands of lives by getting involved in small ways.

Just plant the seed each time one is given to you. This book is a seed... Plant it now!!

Appendix E

Postscript

Now that you have finished this book, I hope you have gained confidence in yourself and your ability. I sincerely hope this book has given you more clarity, understanding, expertise, protection, insight, and opportunity to move further along the path of self-actualization.

I encourage you to use this book as a springboard to action. Your first step from here on out is to go to a major bookstore and gather the rest of the tools that are needed to begin implementing the successful strategies you have chosen to pursue.

Finally, I am asking you to give copies of this book to your family members. Send it across the country to your parents, grandparents, children, grandchildren, aunts, uncles, and friends. For less than $20, you may save them tens of thousands of dollars. People are afraid. You have a tool to diminish fear and maximize potential.

Try to help as many people as you can, in every way possible. We must look out for one another wherever the opportunity exists. That's my personal Magic Bullet and it produces miracles every time it hits its mark.

Please feel free to write, fax, or email me with your thoughts and suggestions concerning this book. If you will provide me with your contact information, I will notify you when the second edition of this book goes to press.

I wish you all the best!

Don't forget to write to tell me your success stories, resulting from this book, I do want to hear from you!

Dan Auito
1619 Three Sisters Way
Kodiak, AK 99615
Fax (907) 481-6300
Email: Dan@magicbullets.com

Appendix F

Getting Raw Land—
Not a Raw Deal!

Just in case you find yourself asking about raw land here is one last little bonus.

Raw land is unimproved property; it has no utilities, sewers, streets, or structures, and usually must be cleared.

There is more to buying raw land than meets the eye and more than a few individuals have wished they'd had a second chance upon finding themselves duped, conned, misled, ill-advised, uninformed, oversold, undereducated, and often unprepared. They realize, often too late, that a raw land purchase should be properly investigated, evaluated, and negotiated using a logical and rational plan.

Let me start by saying I'm not a geologist, soil analyst, surveyor, engineer, or land consultant. I'm a passionate real estate investor, licensed agent, appraisal assistant, and landlord who purchased various raw lots, as large as a 15-acre parcel, for investment and building projects. In addition, I have consulted with numerous individuals proficient in real estate who have contributed to my general awareness of the conditions and merits of raw land. We, as small investors, can further use this information to our advantage in wisely choosing land and utilizing it to its highest and best use regarding fulfillment of our needs, wants, and desires.

This report is not a technical sleeper and as such, it will not go so far as to tell you how much lime to add to your soil to adjust PH levels (7.0 is neutral). What it does do is try to get you thinking about some of the more general considerations that can lead you to further investigate your options using this material as your starting point.

With that said, the first question I'll ask you is: What exactly do you intend to do with this land once you have it? Why are you buying it? What purpose do you have in mind for land? Are you going to build a home? Do you want to purchase a lot for retirement or investment? Will you acquire considerable acreage for farming or subdivision? Do you want commercial, residential, recreational, or agricultural? Will it be in the north, south, east, or west?

So your first question should be: What am I, or we, buying this land for? Will it satisfy my, or our, requirements? To get answers to these questions you would best be served by talking to those who will be most intimately involved with the land, such as your spouse, partner, family members, associated owners, etc. Once you have a clear understanding of what the land is supposed to satisfy, then your search can begin. So often people waste their time and effort because their significant partners have such a wide gap in what each wants from the purchase. They never settle on anything, or end up with much less than they could have had.

Land can be said to consist of soil, geology, water, and climate. Whether you're looking at beaches, mountains, deserts, high plains, or city lots, they all have some basic components. Some of the basic requirements we most often seek are clean air, water, electricity, sewage disposal, and trash removal.

● *Clean air* might be construed as freedom from dusty roads, smog, foul smells from industry or landfills, traffic noise, airports, and neighbors.

• *Water availability* is essential and is often desired for aesthetics as well as drinking, bathing, washing, cooking, cleaning, toilet facilities, and watering vegetation. We also enjoy lakes, rivers, and streams for recreation. Others enjoy the tranquil sounds that our streams, rivers, and oceans can provide. Without a doubt, water availability is a *major* concern. Note: A 1,666 square foot roof can capture 1,000 gallons of water for each inch of rainfall; cisterns of all types have existed since the dawn of man.

• *Electricity* is another necessity we often take for granted. Is a power plant within a reasonable distance from the land or will it cost you thousands of your own dollars to run cables across public lands to get your electricity hooked up? How far are gas and oil suppliers?

• *Sewage disposal.* Twenty-five percent of our country is on a well and septic system. If you don't have access to public utilities, will your land support a septic system as well as the water to operate it?

• *Solid waste disposal.* How far is the landfill? Is there a collection service? You can't burn everything; how will you get rid of it?

Those are the major necessities for modern, everyday living…things we really need but can often overlook until after the contract is signed. Other essentials are a telephone, mail delivery, shopping, police, fire station, hospital/emergency services, schools, churches, recreation facilities, and access by good roads and highways.

You'll want answers to questions like those above. County officials such as planning and zoning, community development, and building departments are good places to start. I would also call utility companies about water, sewer, electric, and phone, and talk to neighbors, contractors, developers, real estate agents, appraisers, and a local surveyor to have some of the more important questions addressed at the beginning of my search. I wouldn't rely on the sellers to be all-knowing either.

Again, planning and zoning departments can offer the following: maps of existing uses, forecasts of future development, lists of planned new roads, utility extensions, locations of planned waste disposal facilities, details on environmental areas and future land uses. They also regulate building codes, curb-cut permits, historic preservation, housing codes, subdivision regulations, tree cutting, and zoning laws. They usually have aerial photographs and plat maps that can help you to better identify and evaluate the land in question.

Do you already have your location identified? Will it be in the East where the weather is often wet and humid or out West where it is predominantly arid and dry? Will you be living in cold weather in the North or gravitating toward the South? Concerning location, what are you least comfortable with: avalanches, landslides, earthquakes, flooding, hurricanes, tornados, tsunamis, volcanoes, and/or wildfires? You may want to investigate areas of interest by going to websites like http://www.officialcitysites. You will get a better picture of what awaits you concerning its economy, environment, and population, plus recreation, educational, medical, and employment facilities, to name a few.

Let's assume you know where you want to buy this land, why you want to buy it, and how and when you will use it once you have it. The following general observations, ideas, and information may help you further investigate the alternatives available to you in your endeavor to find the land of your dreams.

● Some Drawbacks Associated with Raw Land

1. Negative cash flow; usually the land does not generate any income while you pay the principle, interest, taxes, and costs of development.

2. Tax advantages are scanty as land cannot be depreciated.

3. Generally, raw land is considered a long-term ill-liquid investment that often takes time before gains can be realized.

4. Risk of loss on resale can occur if you choose poorly, fail to evaluate and negotiate properly, the economy slips, or various other unforeseen events occur.

5. It is difficult to obtain traditional financing on or borrow against accrued equity.

● Possible Benefits to Raw Land

1. Land has the potential to experience tremendous appreciation if bought in the way of growth, or if a higher and better use can be achieved.

2. Owner financing can often be obtained through the seller at below-market rates.

3. Subdividing can create added value and provide for immediate returns.

4. Privacy and pride of ownership can give the holder a feeling of security.

● What Is Considered Good and Bad Land?

The worst you can buy is swampland or marshland. Most often flat land is the least expensive to develop and the most desirable for building purposes. Land with barren rock will increase costs and virtually eliminate a basement just the same as a high water table.

Note: Loamy soil—which consists of a balanced mixture of clay, sand, and some organic matter and appears rich and dark in color—is considered ideal for most purposes. You don't want hard, cracked ground when dry, or sticky soil when wet. Warning: Check with your state offices for the presence of expansive soils; this stuff cracks foundations in the most insidious ways, leading many to ruin.

Many people are literally being driven to the hills. Granted the views can be spectacular, but roads, utilities, water, sewer, and foundations such as pilings can add 25–30 percent to building costs alone, compounding this already expensive proposition. When considering going vertical, an 8-degree slope is about the limit to build economically on hillsides.

Plots with trees, a view, rectangular shape, a slope from gentle to none, and a good location are most often preferred. Streams can boost values by 100 percent in some cases.

● How to Determine the Value of Raw Land

Using the appraiser's standard view of estimating value can give us some clues, so let's look at what appraisers consider:

- Site size and shape, represented by frontage, width, and depth.
- Corner influence equals visibility for commercial, or privacy for residential.
- Plottage: Has assembly or combining of parcels been accomplished?
- How much land is excess or surplus? Surplus has less value than what is required.
- Topography: land's contour, grading, natural drainage, soil, view, and usefulness.
- Utilities: sewers, drinking water, natural gas, electric, telephone, cable, etc.
- Site improvements: landscaping, fences, gutters, walks, drives, and irrigation.
- Accessibility: parking, location, streets, alleys, connecting roads, and highways.
- Environment: climate, adequate water supply, air quality, streams, rivers, lakes, oceans, and the absence of any hazardous materials.

An old-timer once gave me this advice: "Dan, always try to buy land that is located as close to those amenities that an area is famous for, as that is often the reason people come to certain areas." He lived in Florida and had plenty of beachfront property located in tourist areas, which clearly illustrated his point.

● Who Has This Raw Land and How Do We Find It?

You may start your search by contacting farmers, investors, real estate agents, state and federal agencies, cities with odd lots they need to put back on their tax rolls, bureaus of land management, federal marshals, tax sales, bank foreclosures, developers, property heirs, the elderly, and family and friends. Use your networks and bird dogs while driving areas of interest looking for further opportunities to buy.

Property is often advertised through newspaper ads, real estate brokers, for-sale-by-owner signs, flyers, bulletin boards, the Internet, etc. A quick note on how *not* to buy is in order here. I would not recommend buying land from a glossy brochure or big development company since it is almost always overpriced to cover large overhead costs, advertising, and profit. Also, remember when a building boom is on, land prices rise. You will do much better buying when demand is low. Another caveat is to stay away from land that is advertised outside of its normal market since it is often overpriced or has problems; otherwise, a local buyer would have bought it!

If you want to find the deals, then most often you are going to have to dig for them. A few successful methods may include visiting the county clerk/recorder's office to search the public records for the following:

- New probate filings, use them to contact heirs.
- Eviction proceedings to contact out-of-state landowners.
- Arrests: These people may need money and may also be going away for a while.
- Bail bondsmen who may have forfeited collateral in the form of land.
- Divorces filed, leading to a division of assets.
- New guardianships to contact disinterested heirs.
- Deeds in lieu of foreclosure, private sellers may in turn sell it to you.

● Lis pendens means litigation pending, often signaling fore-closure.

You will most often be contacting many of these sources by writing to them. Don't get discouraged when you don't get immediate replies, since the average response rate is one reply for every eight letters you send. The pros will get on lists and pay services to monitor many of these potential sources; however, good old-fashioned detective work does pay off. When researching in this manner, secrecy is one key and fast action using all cash is the other.

A special consideration to note when hunting legally challenged property is to have a title company in addition to the regular search of mortgage, plus tax and easement liens. Also check files for IRS liens, bankruptcy filings, and judgment liens.

● ● ● ● QUICK REVIEW ● ● ● ●

Up to this point we have talked about not getting conned when starting out. We also noted that it pays to understand what everyone wants from the land to start. You are aware that utilities and basic necessities are very important considerations. You know whom to contact to get further in-depth information on properties of interest. You know flat land with natural amenities is the most desirable and economical to develop. You are more familiar with the risks involved with this type of real estate and you also know that rock, marshes, and hillsides can be expensive to develop. You have a better idea of how an appraiser begins to determine value and you may have a few ideas on how to find land and the people who own it.

With that said, we are ready to get down to the business of evaluating, negotiating, and financing our well-sought piece of terra firma. What follows is a *basic checklist*. There is more to consider but this will get you off to a running start.

● Basic Raw Land Checklist

❑ Get the most recent and valid information available: a copy of the deed containing the legal description with any covenants and/or restrictions.

❑ Get the street address, a plot plan indicating the specific property location, a survey, a preliminary title report, a recent map, and any aerial or land-based photographs to help you locate fence lines, trails, roads, streams, ponds, building locations, etc. Walk the land to verify, evaluate, and correlate what is indicated, also looking for *any* signs of hazardous waste dumping, burying, or burning.

❑ Determine present use in zoning, according to what planning and zoning tells you. Symbols are used to designate uses. Here are a few:

    A1: Agricultural with single family home
    C: Commercial business
  CO: Commercial office
    FP: Flood plain
    M: Industrial
    R1: Residential single family
 R1H: Residential hillside
    R2: Residential multifamily
    RT: Recreational tourist/residential transitional

General categories include:
- ● Farm, ranch, and timberland
- ● Recreational or resort
- ● Industrial
- ● Commercial/business
- ● Residential
- ● Mixed use

1. Confirm who owns it, their full name, address, and phone number.
2. Find out what they do; are they a dealer in real estate?
3. Ask if anyone else is on the title or has authority to act.
4. What are the annual taxes and assessed values?
5. Ask why they are selling and how long they have owned it.
6. If the owner doesn't want to sell, ask if they would consider selling a parcel of it.

The Basic Raw Land Checklist is an abbreviated tool to start you off on the right foot. Many people will research buying a new car more thoroughly than they would raw land; there are many good books that are devoted solely to the subject of raw land. This type of investment is generally not the best choice for the new investor but often people look to build their dream home away from developed areas. For that reason I have included my two cents here.

● Finance Considerations

Raw land, as opposed to improved property, is much more difficult to finance through traditional lenders. The main reasons are that it generates very little income, development costs can be expensive, there are no buildings or improvements that can be used as collateral, and it is often considered speculative. Therefore we find that sellers are often our first choice regarding financing.

It is typical for a seller of raw land to accept 10 percent down and the rest to be paid over time at a specified (below market) interest rate. This would be an example of an installment land contract. Other forms are contract for deed, mortgage and note, and purchase money mortgages. In these cases, a real estate attorney usually drafts these contracts and a bank will act as an escrow agent to facilitate verifiable records of payments received. The seller often retains the deed until the property is paid for in full.

If you want to investigate bank financing, then you may start out by offering 30 percent down with a 7-year mortgage, with the bank getting an extra percentage point over and above the current interest rates for standard loans. This may not be accepted but it does give you a starting point to see just what they may be willing to do.

If you plan on building on your land, then having a development plan with an appraised set of blueprints for the project will help the lender in justifying your loan. If you can use equity from other property, then paying substantial down payments may also be an option.

My final words of caution here would be to *know values* and don't overpay. Always offer less when possible and research recent sales of comparable properties. The larger a parcel is, the cheaper it tends to get per acre. Ask an agent what an acre of land tends to go for in the area you are considering. Try to buy more than one acre.

When buying residential lots, builders try to keep raw land costs down to 10 percent of the overall value of the project. If streets and utilities are already in place, then they will use 25 percent as their guideline. If you can combine or assemble parcels or achieve zoning changes with property, you have a good chance of immediately increasing its value. Always physically inspect the property and do your research *before* obligating yourself to buy it. Try using contracts with contingencies put in to protect you. In essence, these are options that let you control the deal while you investigate and research the land's potential to satisfy your objectives.

Happy Hunting and buy the high grounds!

BONUS REPORT

Magic Bullets
Kill Sacred Cows

A For Sale by Owner Outline

(This report can be found at www.magicbullets.com, fully customized and hyperlinked for your internet surfing pleasure, please feel free to forward it to your friends and family!)

Dear Reader:

Because of the loss of control of proprietary information and systems, the ability to project great power and control are being lost at a most alarming rate. For many, the World Wide Web is delivering devastating blows to those who seek to keep information and methods of operation private, while at the same time the Internet collects, integrates, connects, multiplies, stores, and delivers what was once private to millions with the click of a mouse. Today, experts give control, they don't horde it!

New global intellectual capital know-how has emerged on the Web; disintermediation is fast becoming the watch word that signals the end of the 20th century middleman. The person who once bridged the chasm between buyer and seller is being replaced by the synapse of a new hyperlinked marketplace that renders service with lightning-fast speed.

There is a goldmine of information at our fingertips but we still have a few minor problems to address before we search for Internet gold. Our primary concern is how to find, organize, and put into practical use our newfound ore.

As you may have noticed, we begin our journey at the third crossroad of human evolution. We've already passed through the agricultural age of the 1800s and our second revolutionary shift of mechanized mass production of the 1900s is also behind us. Here then we begin our journey into the information age, the new millennium of the 2000s and beyond.

Throughout the rest of this section, we'll be traveling at electrified speeds—so hold on tight. We will be traveling to all places real estate related on the net while attempting to educate some friends along the way. Please allow me to introduce myself: My name is Figment and I will be your driver, guide, and concierge throughout our journey together.

Let's pull in and get acquainted with our guest, shall we?

"Excuse me, friend. Did you put a call into the cyber-line network?"

"Yes, sir, I did. Are you the concierge?"

"Yes, indeed, I am. My name is Figment. Might I ask your name?"

"My name is Fizbo, but you can call me Fiz."

"That's a fine name. Won't you get in?

"It would be my pleasure, Figment."

"Just call me Fig!"

"Fig it is! I'm sure glad to see you and it's a pleasure to meet you."

"Likewise!"

"What's all the to-do about, Fiz? Sounds like you have some concerns."

"Well, Fig, I've been searching endlessly for answers to a few real estate questions and the subject seems to overwhelm me at times. I've been reading, randomly surfing the Internet, and asking questions, but nothing seems to make sense. I can't get a straight answer from anyone and some folks have downright tried to take advantage of my situation."

"Wahoo, that's a real knee-slapper, Fiz. I've got just the cure. Let's get started, shall we?"

"I'm ready when you are, Fig!"

"All right, then here's the before takeoff briefing. We'll need to bring you up to speed so we can all function as a team. And 'team' stands for *together everyone achieves more!*"

As you've probably noticed, we're driving a sleek Dell 8300 with a 2.6-gig power plant today, and we've got her turbocharged with a Web-linked cable modem as well. Fiz, we'll be traveling at astonishing speeds to our destinations on the information highway so it's critical that we know where we're going and how we're going to get there.

Our three main expressways are **www.google, www.yahoo,** and **www.vivisimo.** There are some side streets but these will do for today. Other than that, Fiz, just remember that good manners are your best insurance policy in cyberspace.

Where would you like to go today? You ordered the guided tour package, didn't you? According to your profile here, it says you're going to be selling a home soon and you want to do this without the help of 20th century middlemen. We need to get you caught up to speed on current market conditions and what's really going on in the environment concerning real estate.

I have a friend who can help us out with that. I've made arrangements for you to speak with Brad at **www.inman.com.** He knows a lot about what's going on with real estate. Please, let's all go in, shall we?

It looks as though rates are holding steady for now, but come the end of summer I expect they'll begin to rise. This may bring us more foreclosures and fewer buyers at lower prices because of the cost of funds. Thanks, Brad; that tells us we'd better keep moving or we may miss a great seller's market. We'll have a look around and keep in touch.

BRAD'S PLACE:
REAL ESTATE INDUSTRY NEWS HEADLINE

Mortgage rates rise on good job news
Fed may hike up key funds rate as soon as summer

Foreclosure real estate could be good find
Web site offers information for property investors   *continued . . .*

Real estate: The week ahead
Not-to-miss industry events

Will telling truth cost me my first big sale?
Representation includes giving buyer unwanted advice, ethicist says

Overnight mortgage rates rise
30-year fixed up at 5.23 percent; 10-year treasury up at 3.89 percent

Real estate agents fight for paid search spots
Keyword competition heats up between local, national advertisers

Wow, that guy Brad really has his finger on the pulse of national real estate news, Fig. Let's stop in to see Ian at www.thepaperboy.com to get today's digital paper from your local area, Fiz. We'll need to see what's going on in your neck of the woods to get perspective. Here's a map, compliments of www.mapquest.com. Let's use it to get to Fiz's neighborhood.

Very nice, Fiz, you live in a great area here. Why exactly are you selling anyway?

Well, Fig, to be honest, I was offered a better position within our company but I'll have to transfer out west if I want the position. Our company is expanding to fill the demand for new services in that area. Seven thousand new people moved to Las Vegas just last month alone.

That's interesting, Fiz, kind of makes you think of those aging baby boomers like a golf ball in a garden hose all heading for greener pastures.

Yes, Fig, we're also expanding into Florida, California, and Texas. Our pharmaceutical sales are going through the roof!

Pardon me for a moment. Would you mind if we took a better look at these trends? Let's zip over to www.census.gov for a moment to get the big picture. Fig, look at this! If you go to the resources section and click www.fedstats.gov/qf/ it points you to demographics and statistics on any state you choose and http://www.census.gov/hhes/ww/housing/ahs/ahs01/tab1a3.html breaks down housing statistics across the entire country!

Listen to this, Fig, it says in **http://www.census.gov/prod/2002pubs/censr-4.pdf** that over the next two decades the number of Americans 65 and over is expected to double from 35 million to 70 million. They also say that 13 million foreign-born people settled in the United States in the 1990s. Gee wiz, we only had 76 million in 1900; that figure has almost quadrupled in the last 100 years to 293 million today. They go on to say that by 2050 we'll be up to 420 million and by 2100 we can expect to have 570 million. That's almost twice the number we have today. Where will they all live?

That's a trillion-dollar question. Maybe we should pull up **www.globelexplorer.com** to pinpoint tracts of land to buy between existing cities that we'll need for another 120 million homes in the future. All right, it's time to go. We can't let ourselves be lured into the Web. We must remain focused by coming to get what we came for and then continuing on our way.

Fiz, I suppose it's time we get down to business here. You requested an overview of real estate in general, so we've looked at the past, present, and future regarding those issues. You are certainly welcome to investigate further but our time together is limited so we must move on. Your second and most pressing need expressed is that you would like to sell your present home without the assistance of the 20th century middleman—in other words, by owner.

Okay, Fiz, let's take stock of where we've been so that we use what we've found to help us do the work we're about to do. Let's get perspective! We began our journey by saying the agricultural era and industrial age are behind us. Today we find ourselves flush with the capacity to link to all sources of intelligence and resources across the globe and beyond. No one owns the Internet, therefore, no one can withhold the flow of information to those who seek it. In 1950, half the population were renting; today three-quarters of the population own their own homes. One in five sellers sold their own homes last year, closer to one in four will do it this year and that number is sure to grow with 17,280 homes sold every day of the year.

Now close your eyes, Fiz and hold out your hand. I've just given you a fist full of Magic Bullets. You can't see them, but you can use them when you need to. These bullets have been carefully crafted and proven to work for thousands of years, so do not discount them just because you can't see them. Many people will tell you that they don't exist and here is your first lesson.

● Lesson 1: They Exist When You *Believe* They Do. *Belief* Is Bullet One!

How do I shoot them, Fig?

Well, Fiz, you'll need to craft your own firearm to actually use these bullets with any great success.

But, Fig, I can't even see them, how in the world—?

Attitude, Fiz! The weapon that fires Magic Bullets is a *positive mental attitude*.

How do I get that, Fig?

If you will mix faith, hope, and desire with hard work and enthusiasm, I believe you will find the result most accurate and accommodating. Now let's move on, remember we must remain focused. I'll be introducing you to some new friends along the way here in our second part of the journey, so if everyone's ready? We'll start off by removing the number 1 *fear* in most people's minds when it comes to doing it yourself, that being the legal side of the process.

Good news, fellow travelers; the world has changed. You, as a seller of your own personal as well as real property, are granted by our constitution the right to sell, barter, trade, or otherwise dispose of your property in any way you see fit, so long as it doesn't interfere with the rights of others or cause them harm. What this really says is that you could literally write a contract on a napkin and if all elements are present and in writing, a court of law would enforce it. These are the things that must be present or considered in order for your napkin to stand up in court:

1. *Offer and acceptance.* You must have a written agreement between seller and purchaser in which the purchaser agrees to buy certain real estate and the seller agrees to sell upon terms of agreement. This is the basis of your contract for sale. This must be in writing to satisfy the law of "the statute of frauds." That law says oral contracts for real estate are unenforceable.

2. *Seal or consideration.* A person's signature in this case does satisfy the requirement of promising to go through with the deal as agreed but almost all sellers rely on a cold, hard earnest money deposit to ensure the other party is, in fact, earnest. I would accept 1 percent of the value of the property in the form of an earnest money check as a fair amount of consideration to further deal with a well-qualified party at hand. This check is often written in the name of a third "neutral" party to hold in trust, such as a lawyer, title officer, or other official party.

3. *Capacities of the parties.* Examples of incompetence may be minors, mentally incompetents, insane persons, people under the influence of drugs or alcohol, corporate officers unauthorized to contract, and so forth. Foreigners from other nations have full contractual authority, but federal law prohibits you from selling to the enemy. The person with whom you are contracting must have contractual capacity.

4. *Reality of consent.* A contract must be free of mistakes, misrepresentation, fraud, duress, and undue influence. You can't legally describe one property as the one a person is buying and then when the deal is done they find that the actual property purchased is the shack next door.

5. *Legality of the object.* The object of the contract must be legal. If the purpose violates the constitution, a statute, or federal treaty or law, the contract is void. In other words, if you contract to buy illicit drugs and the other party doesn't deliver, don't expect the courts to uphold your agreement.

Did you get all that, Fiz? That's not so hard, is it? Find a reasonable person who wants to buy your house. Don't lie, and get the details in writing backed by their good-faith deposit. Now you can iron out any contingencies or details that need to be taken care of to get the job done.

For all the reasons stated above, I cannot emphasize enough how extremely important it is to write the following words on every contract you ever sign: *This entire agreement is subject to my attorney's approval.* Don't alter the above sentence in any way—unless your attorney tells you to do so.

A good real estate attorney will give you all the paperwork you need according to the laws in your state. These often include the following:

● A sales contract

● An earnest money agreement

● A property transfer disclosure, lead paint disclosure, predator disclosures (Megan's Law), and so forth

● A bill of sale for personal property that will convey washers, dryers, refrigerators, and so forth

An attorney also will review all the details while consulting with you all the way up to and including accompanying you to the closing, usually for a $500 to $750 flat fee. Your lawyer is your first material Magic Bullet. He or she will also assist you in becoming "bulletproof" yourself.

FINDING AN ATTORNEY

www.attorneyfinder.com/index.html
http://www.turnpike.net/lawnet/forum.mv?post+1
(Questions are answered here for free.)
www.audrie.com (You will grow to love this woman.)

Below, are some additional resources.

CONTRACTS/FORMS SUPPLIERS

www.audrie.com
www.uslegalforms.com

www.kaktus.com
www.urgentbusinessforms.com
www.standardlegal.net
www.isoldmyhouse.com/forms.html (free contracts)
www.eHow.com (then follow finance to real estate)
www.phoenixfsbos.com/forms_contracts.html (free contracts)
www.mortgage-investments.com/Real_estate_and_mortgage_ Forms/form_fr.htm (free)
www.findlaw.com (back out of page, pop-up allows free access)
www.alllaw.com/forms/real_estate (sample forms and lawyer search)
www.attorneylocate.com/index.html
  (sample forms and lawyer search)
www.homefindersbulletin.com/docs/checklist.pdf
  (free tenant move-in checklist)
www.thelpa.com/lpa/free-forms.html?id=nyy2upaZ
  (free landlord forms)
www.legalscholar.com/links/realestateassociations.html (law resource)

You now have the law on your side and a professional who can practice it to your advantage. We have much to do, Fiz. How you feeling so far?

I'm with you, Fig. What am I going to do next?

Fiz, as you can see my first task with you was to remove your *fear*, so I think that is what we must address when we ask others to buy our homes. In reality, when we're done here they'll more than likely be begging you to sell it to them.

That brings me to a point that few realize. Sure, you're selling land and all the things that are affixed to it, which includes a bundle of rights. That's a general definition of real property, but what you're really doing is attempting to transfer the *power* that object represents. People often are searching for a trouble-free, pleasurable, aesthetically pleasing, comfortable, needs-fulfilling, safe, secure, affordable, and convenient place to live. This, my friend, is what sells homes for top dollar in almost all cases. It works for rentals, too. Until you address those concerns one by one, you're going to have unresolved *fears*, which will make your job much harder than it ever needs to be.

● Lesson 2: Remove as Much *Fear* as You Can From Your Buyer's Mind.

How do I do that, Fig?

You already have the proper paperwork and an attorney who will ensure everyone is treated fairly according to the real estate laws of your state. That alone relieves the buyers of the thought of how the details of paperwork will be handled. It is your job to prove to them that you can be trusted to transfer your *power* to them effectively.

You may as well round up as many of the following documents as you can, as they will be used in many ways to help you in marketing your home and effectively transferring power over it. Organized effort is another Magic Bullet!

(Tip: When you begin the task of collecting as many of the documents below as you can, it pays to contact a local title company—or better yet the one who is named on your title policy first to get a property profile or ownership and encumbrance report [O&E]. A title company can provide copies of warrantee deeds and mortgage notes, and alert you to any assessments, mechanics' liens, or unpaid taxes. They may also have surveys and plot plans revealing encroachments and so forth. This property profile helps to give your property's legal title status a clean bill of health. Get one, if you can, and add it to the list below. Deals fall through when defects [clouds] on the title aren't cleared up early. Get your attorney early on to get this done.)

Organized effort is another Magic Bullet! Let's take a look at the list:

- ● The appraisal
- ● The inspection report
- ● The home warranty
- ● Sales contracts
- ● Property disclosure sheets
- ● Any preliminary title review documents
- ● Copy of your survey
- ● Current title policy

● A copy of your warranty deed
● Your latest real estate tax statement
● One year's worth of utility bills
● Copies of any deed restrictions and homeowner's association rules, plus all home and appliance warranties.
● A pest inspection report
● Any permits pulled for modifications done
● Well flow and septic percolation tests, if applicable

Appraisal? Fig, I thought the buyers paid for that and their lender called an approved appraiser from their own list.

Relax, Fiz, you're right. Normally the buyer pays and the lender calls for and gets the report. You're going to use this twist to great advantage.

APPRAISAL

www.appraisalfoundation.com (click on ".ORG")
www.appraisalinstitute.com/default.asp (find your appraiser)
www.naifa.com (find another)
www.appraisersforum.com/forum/index.php (ask an appraiser)
www.electronicappraiser.com (general valuations)
www.camerondirect.com/compsources.shtml (comparable data)
www.Realtor.com (your local competition displayed)

Assuming you have an attorney picked out, your home inspected, repaired, and prepared to show at its best, it's time to call the appraiser. You want to, in effect, sell the home's finer points to the appraiser, let him or her know of the upgrades and special features of the home, and so forth. Most appraisers are mathematicians and number-crunching geniuses. Don't expect them to spend all day jabbering with you. They take their jobs seriously and don't miss much, so don't patronize them or you could do more harm than good! Give them the facts and get out of the way.

There are many ways and places to collect information that will help you to determine a most probable selling price. The best way to start is to begin talking to your neighbors, especially those who are in the process of selling themselves (go to the open houses listed in your local newspaper). These other sellers may be your competition but they have no idea that you are theirs. Brokers or their agents will give you a comparative market analysis for free but will be checking in quite regularly to see if you're ready to give in to their way of thinking.

For residential property, appraisers follow this general line of thought: The *comparable approach* is most often used in single-family home valuation. The appraiser takes three or more houses that are similar in style/design, size, quality, age, and neighborhood, preferably within a mile of each other, that have sold within the last six months to a year. They then make adjustments for better or worse features to the comparables to arrive at a probable sales price of the house that is being appraised. This approach is based on the principle of substitution, which says no one would pay more for something that they could get for a lesser amount somewhere else (within a mile or so).

Appraisals generally run from $300 to $500 for today's standard 2,200-square-foot home. The odds are good that your buyers are going to have their lender already picked out by the time they find you, and it's also likely that their lender will have to call for another appraisal from an approved appraiser on their list. This is fine because you used your appraisal to convince your buyers that your house was fairly priced, and your appraisal helped to remove their *fear* of paying too much. It also helped you to squelch bargain hunters' comments that you were asking too much. It paid for itself, believe me! Now if you were happy with your appraiser's opinion of value, you may consider letting the lender's appraiser have a copy as he or she will most likely use the same comparables. You've made it easy for them!

INSPECTION RESOURCES

www.inspectamerica.com (free inspection outline)
www.ashi.com (find a home inspector)
www.homeinspections.com (thousands of inspectors)
www.independentinspectors.org (ditto)
www.nachi.org/bbsystem/index.php (ask a home inspector)
www.inspectorsjournal.com (ditto)

Having the home inspection done before the appraiser is ever called can help you obtain a higher appraisal. You can also relieve the *fear* in the appraiser's mind as well, and he or she won't be holding back escrowed funds from your valuations for mandatory repairs that must be made before the appraisal will fly through the lenders underwriting department.

While you are accompanying the home inspector on his or her inspection, you should be taking notes as well. As you go along, you will also see things that need cleaning, oiling, tightening, adjusting, replacing, and so forth. Just jot them down on your own pad while you stay close to the inspector, paying close attention to his or her recommendations and insights along the way. Between the inspector's list and your own, you will be well on your way to eliminating any unforeseen problems. Don't forget to stop by Frank's place at **www.inspectamerica.com** to print a free copy of a great inspection outline to use during your own walk around.

As we said from the beginning, we are going to remove as much *fear* from the buyers as we can. By getting our own inspection done before we show the home, we have time to find and correct any and all defects beforehand. I see it all the time. When buyers get their own inspector he or she finds things that you should have found and other things you had no idea were wrong. In some cases, the codes have changed so what was once acceptable is now a major issue. With this kind of ammunition the buyers more often than not are able to negotiate strongly to get price concessions from you, and their *fear* has been justified! You can't let that happen.

By getting your own inspection first, everything will be found, fixed, and brought up to code long before the buyers start looking. There won't be a delay in your closing date either, waiting to get those things fixed. Once you have the report, fix what was found wrong and keep the receipts with the bound report. You'll be showing it to the perspective buyers. Ideally you want them to accept your report at face value; if the buyers still have *fear*, then you should encourage them to call the inspector whose name is on the report.

I will give you a few tips of my own on how to prepare your home completely inside and out to present the absolute best possible appeal but as you are seeing, it makes no sense to do something twice when you can easily go direct to a source who will give you excellent advice for free. Now off you go, Fiz, to http://www.audrie.com/Preparing_a_house.htm. Also pay attention to Audrie's additional resources in the left sidebar. Many sites have this information in their resources. Just look under "resources," you're sure to find it!

HOME IMPROVEMENT
www.hometime.com (plan your work)
www.diyonline.com (remodel it)
www.doityourself.com (super site)
www.plbg.com (plumbing repair forum)
www.paintcenter.org/pexpertqa1.cfm (the world of paint)
www.decoratorsecrets.com (finishing touches)
www.forums.gardenweb.com/forums/#subs (the garden)

We have one last key to the puzzle of *fear* removal and then you can prepare to advertise this properly priced, absolutely flawless home to the world. The last *fear* removal tool is *a home warranty*; this too will be paid for by you. They run about $400 for a one-year policy and protect you as well as transferring to the new owners when the sale closes.

HOME WARRANTY
www.homewarrantyexperts.com (find a good warranty company)
www.orhp.com (home warrantees)

Purchase the home warranty last as you now have proof that the systems that will be protected under the agreement have been inspected and have no existing defects that would void the coverage.

So far we have paid for:

An attorney	$750
A home inspection	$300
An appraisal	$400
A home warranty	$400
Total	$1,850

How will this save us money? Let's first take something you may not have considered into our overall plan to get top dollar. Not many people remove this much *fear* in the process of selling their home. Many sellers are completely unprepared for what is in store for them. On top of this, three out of four sellers (your supposed competition) are using brokers or their agents, who on average charge a 6 percent commission for what you are doing yourself.

Using the median average home sale price of $183,500 (as of 2004 census statistics) multiplied by 6 percent or .06 x $183,500 = $11,010, subtract your $1,850 from that and you are left with a savings of $9,160. Now the killer here is that your supposed competition hasn't provided a single solitary *fear* removal tool.

You have actually saved the buyers potentially another $1,100 for those items—not to mention the time! You are now in a superior position of power. And this does not take into consideration that homes prepared like yours are what generally tend to drive prices higher, so you may be setting a new benchmark (higher price) in your neighborhood because of the way you have prepared and marketed your home. It is not out of the question that you could move your neighborhood's overall values up by, say, a modest 3 percent or $5,505, as a result of providing all this value.

Add the $5,505 to your $9,160 and your real savings may just be $14,665 on your average home sale of $183,500. That's a 12.5 percent overall gain, not a 6 percent loss paid in the form of a commission. Add those together and you've effectively repositioned yourself 18.5 percent better than most traditional sellers will end up. Silicon Valley homes average $600,000. What's 18.5 percent of that? (It's $111,000, to be exact.) This is not theory, my friend. I do it and sell for $10,000 more than similar homes. People are astounded by this. You see it, plan for it, and achieve it! I hope you can see how setting these dominos up like we have so far can really pay off.

There are cases when a paid professional will get the business. Here are some prime examples:

1. The owner is out of the area and cannot do it personally.
2. The owner is being relocated and their company is paying all costs.
3. The owners are uncomfortable with the process involved with showing, contracts, and so forth.
4. The owners make tons of money and their time is more valuable than the commission.
5. The owners don't have the time to do it themselves.

(Note: The average full service real estate commission is now 5.12 percent. [This is not set in stone, it's just an average.] Of the 40 percent of people who asked for a lower commission rate 74 percent were successful. Learn to negotiate by using the *ask* principle. [If you don't ask, you won't receive!])

Those are good reasons to give it to a pro; however, let's take a time out here and listen in on some brokers or their agents talking about what is going on in the industry.

Original Excerpts

Steven writes: "Well, I know by all of you out there that this was happening across the country, and now it's here in Rhode Island. I spoke to two FSBOs today. Both told me they were listing their properties on the MLS for $300. The broker does *nothing*.

"Now I know how some of you are feeling. This goes against everything a broker stands for and the local MLS should *not* allow this to take place.

"So what's happening out there in some of your areas. Have any local MLSs stopped this?"

Alice comments: "Steve, this is allowed in our MLS—plus they advertise it on LARGE SIGN BOARDS! (Yes, I am yelling.) Go to **www.nuwaymls.com**. We also have a place where they can buy a spot on MLS for a flat fee. Feel the rope tightening?"

Mark responds: "This is happening in my area as well. Whenever times are good for sellers, you see this sort of thing. Historically, none of these entities lasts because ultimately they don't price at a level to maintain themselves as a long-term going concern. These entities jump in to soak up what economists would call 'excess profits.' They come and then they go. It's *no* big deal!"

There's a bigger issue here. How do you think about those entities and how effective are you in communicating that thinking to consumers of your services? (Fear, Fiz.)

FSBOs can put a sign up and FSBOs can advertise in the local newspapers. FSBOs can put up their property on a Web site. FSBOs can send out postcards to the neighborhood and all the people they know. Now FSBOs can get into MLS and the Web sites that are fed by MLS. FSBOs have almost all the tools that highly trained brokers or their agents have. So what! (Did you hear that, Fiz?)

This weekend Home Depot will be packed with salespeople and accountants and meat cutters and housewives and the full assortment of people who don't know what they are doing; all buying tools and supplies to work on their properties. I'll be in the tile department buying some tile with a long-time friend— a guy who started setting tile 40 years ago at his father's knee. And his father learned tile setting from *his* father. All of the tools of the trade, besides a couple of diamond saws, fit in a 5-gallon bucket. At the same time we are there, there will certainly be one or more young gals or guys also buying tile and mastic. Who do you think will have the better result in the shorter period of time? Who do you think will better handle the problems that inevitably arise in a tile setting job? Who would *you* rather have setting your tiles if you were interested in getting the best long-term result? (6 percent x $183,500 = $11,010—a very expensive tile guy).

Access to the tools of the trade is important but not as important as being able to operate those tools. It isn't the tools that are important in getting a property sold near or at the top of the market values range but the knowledge, skill, and experience of the person *using* those tools. That is the answer to this recurring but fleeting occurrence in our business. (Use the knowledge, skill, and experience of the combined world—the Internet, Fiz!) What this means is that either you do this right or don't do it at all.

You see, Fiz, this is really a battle for control. If you don't control your own destiny, someone else will!

Let's move on. Here is another point in the selling of a home that strikes *fear* in the minds of those who do not do it every day. Who pays for what closing costs? Relax, Fiz, you're going to look like the good guy here because you already paid for the attorney, appraisal, inspection, and home warranty. This makes the buyer easier to deal with when it comes to negotiating who pays what. They already see you as generous, and they, in turn, should accept what you have decided beforehand.

As the seller, your costs are generally much lower than the buyer's since you do not generally pay for the following:

● Loan application fees
● Credit report fees
● Loan origination fees
● Lender's documentation and preparation fees
● Prepaid interest
● Insurance escrows and reserves for taxes
● A lender's insurance title policy premium
● Property transfer taxes

Plus, you may have saved them from having to pay for an appraisal, a home inspection, and some title closing fees as a result of your lawyer's participation.

The above fees, which often equal 2.5 percent to 3 percent (variable) of the loan amount itself before any required down payments, really put the burden on the buyer's side of the closing statement.

As the seller, you may reasonably expect to pay some of the following:

- Broker's commission (Not happening!)
- Your existing mortgage balance to your original lender
- Recording fee to record the mortgage payoff above and clear the title
- Prorated taxes to the buyers from the first of the year to closing date
- Half of the traditional closing costs
- Tax service fees
- Owner's title insurance policy
- Property survey
- Miscellaneous recording fees
- Pest, radon, lead, asbestos, water, roof, mechanicals, and local inspection fees
- Other city or state fees
- All expenses of the FSBO, marketing, signage, ads, Internet listing fees, and so forth

Your attorney is going to explain it all. You should sit down when you go to get your forms from the attorney and decide shortly thereafter what you are willing to pay for and what you expect the buyers to pay. Many items fall under the guise of traditional charges and many can also be split. As a baseline under this outline here, you can figure about 1 percent of your sales price for closing costs. On a $200,000 home that would be about $2,000 in closing costs (not including your secret weapons), some higher, some lower. These are deducted out of your sales proceeds—the closing check!

Since I am not in a position to know your state's particular customs and the specific details of your transaction, it is an absolute requirement that you consult with your attorney, title officer, lenders, and especially the buyers involved with the transaction to ensure you and everyone else are properly advised and prepared for your settlement day. By getting involved in the details in this active way, you will gain a much better understanding of the process and learn far more than three out of four sellers do in most cases. (You will become a smarter buyer too!)

FINANCIAL

www.mortgagemag.com/mo1534.htm (mortgage discussion)

http://www.calcbuilder.com/cgi-bin/calcs/HOM9.cgi/mbaa (closing cost calculators)

www.interest.com (financial/loans)

www.eloan.com (another)

www.mortgagequotes.com (another)

www.quickenmortgage.com (another)

www.mortgage-referral.com (another)

www.lendingleaders.com (another)

www.bankrate.com (today's rates and more)

www.bankrate.com/brm/mortgage-calculator.asp (calculator) Excellent!

www.mortgage101.com (calculators and more)

www.homefair.com (calculators and relocation information)

www.homebuyingguide.com/default.asp ("4free" finance books) PDF

Moving right along, let's look at our list again:

● The appraisal
● The inspection report
● The home warranty
● Sales contracts
● Property disclosure sheets
● Copy of your survey
● Current title policy
● A copy of your warranty deed
● Your latest real estate tax statement
● One year worth of utility bills
● Copies of any deed restrictions, homeowner's association rules plus all home and appliance warranties
● A pest inspection report
● Any permits pulled for modifications done
● Well flow and septic percolation tests, if applicable

At this point we have the big things pretty much out of the way: You have an attorney, the home inspection, the appraisal, the home warranty and your sales contracts along with what you are willing to pay toward closing costs. The rest of the documents below will seal your case and blow *fear* clear off the table and out the door. All of these documents will be laid out in order on a display table before we are done, and the prospective buyers will be able to review every detail that they need to eliminate any questions that lead to *fear,* which ultimately kills deals. Let's get the rest of these documents below and effectively transfer the *power* of ownership to those new owners.

● *Property disclosure form*

This simply outlines all the things that make up the home, its systems, and the land that it rests upon. Your job is to fill in the blanks telling the truth about everything a new owner should know, including any material defects that you know of that have existed or still do. Your attorney will give you your state's outline and you simply answer the questions as best you can. It's not pass or fail; just be honest and you're done. Now put that one in the pile of things we have completed. (You may look at this one for ideas **www.isoldmyhouse.com/forms.html**.)

● *Copy of your survey*

The seller almost always pays for this; you should have a copy with your original closing documents from when you bought the home. If not, the county tax records office usually has it on file. If you cannot find it or you have added additions or outbuildings, a swimming pool, fencing, and so forth, you will need to get a new survey ordered from a local surveyor's office. Check the local phone book or get a referral to a surveyor in your area. (See **www.landsurveyors.com**.)

● *Current title policy*

This document is part of your original closing paperwork; you will need this to prove that you are protected against title defects and claims against your ownership or title to the property. It's just a form of proof (insurance policy) that you own what you're selling and are also protected against claims. You will use it to get a very accurate legal description when we do your facts and features sheets for the big sales event. Hint: Have your attorney perform a preliminary review of title and get a written statement that the title has been reviewed and is in order. (Remove *fear*.)

● *Copy of your warranty deed*
Keep your original safe. This too can be found in your original closing documents. It simply states that you are the owner of the property and all rights associated with that property as well. This is a recorded document and can also be found in public records or at the title company. Provide a display copy for your perspective buyer's perusal.

● *Latest tax statement*
This shows what your property is assessed at for tax purposes and what your annual tax is on the property. It also is another form of proof that you own the property. This helps buyers to begin to figure what there tax liability will be. The mill rate multiplied by the sale price determines the annual tax bill due as a result of the sale. By visiting your local tax office you can get all documentation on file for your home free.

● *One year's worth of utility bills*
This lessens the *fear* of the unknown by showing people what they can expect. This allows them to plan, compare, and evaluate the actual costs for water, sewer, trash, electric, gas, oil, cable rates, and so forth. If you make a contact list for all the providers above, your buyers will see that as a time-saving, value-added document. It costs you zero to add this value.

● *Pest inspection reports and city approvals*
Termite reports are mandatory in many southern states; other states require the fire marshal to approve of smoke detectors and other safety issues they may deem of importance. Get these reports and approvals beforehand so you can display them proudly.

● *Energy ratings and appliance documents*

Many lenders today base loan rates on a home's energy rating as it takes into account the quality of the home's construction and materials used. Include warranties and receipts for every appliance that will remain with the home—refrigerator, stove, dishwasher, washer/dryer, garage door opener with remotes, well and pool pumps, sprinkler systems and timers, electronic thermostats, heating and air conditioners, dehumidifiers, water softeners, jet tubs, disposals, faucets, security systems, and so forth. With every document you find, you stack the deck in your favor!

● *Copies of rules and regulations*

Gather all documents that explain any deed restrictions, association rules and regulations, annual or monthly dues or fees, plus approvals required to lease or sell for condos and townhomes.

● *Information sheets are your facts and features sheets*

Using all the above items plus our inspection reports and appraisal combined with the following information, we are going to build a facts and features sheet that will blow your buyers away. We leave nothing to chance; we plan, orchestrate, deliver, and win. You're creating a tidal wave of benefits that will flow to the right buyer in the market who finds your home first.

● *Timeout*

When talking to sellers about their home, real estate agents will most often refer to it as a "house" to condition them to emotionally detach themselves from the object. When they're talking to buyers, it becomes a "home." You need to get this mind-set; it's an emotional point and emotion is what sells everything in this world.

You must detach yourself emotionally from the home you will be leaving, while at the same time presenting it to the buyers in a warm light that says this is a wonderful home that will bring you much, comfort, joy, happiness, security, and wealth. Your job is to put feeling into your advertising; you have already removed the *fear* so now we focus on all the benefits, prestige, security, and happiness that come with buying this home.

HOME IMPROVEMENT
www.hometime.com (plan your work)
www.diyonline.com (remodel it)
www.doityourself.com (super site)
www.plbg.com (plumbing repair forum)
www.paintcenter.org/pexpertqa1.cfm (the world of paint)
www.decoratorsecrets.com (finishing touches)
www.forums.gardenweb.com/forums/#subs (the garden)

The sites above show how to find, fix or repair, and evaluate which improvements to make regarding your home's overall appearance.

Don't underestimate the importance of curb appeal. You could have done everything right, but the appearance from the street often sends people on their way without even stepping up to your door. Your advertising may have made them envision something completely different from what actually exists. We will ensure you do this right by having you write your advertising after you fill out your facts and features sheets. This way you will accurately describe exactly what you're offering directly to your target audience.

We also gathered all those documents first so that you can now use them to pull all the information that you'll need to write an effective ad. Fiz, assuming you have or soon *will* have new paint, carpet, wood, tile, or vinyl in neutral earth-tone colors where needed, everything repaired or replaced—including those old toilet seats, the interior surfaces of the home so clean you would eat off them, the rooms so clutter free you could play racquetball, the windows so clear birds fly into them, the yard so manicured you could spot a bottle cap from 50 feet away, all your documents collected and ready to access like an IRS auditor on the hunt for a tax-dodging drug lord, I believe we are ready to create your facts and features sheets.

But first, three more Magic Bullets coming at you:

1. Your facts and features sheets
2. Your advertising campaign and showing instructions
3. Closing techniques to get you on your way

● The Facts and Features Sheets (The More You Tell, the More You Sell)

www.bestplaces.net/ (city and school facts and more)
www.nhfind.com (community info)
www.usacitylink.com (relocation guide to cities)
www.50states.com (state facts & info)
www.searchbug.com (find people, places, and things)
www.realtytimes.com (market conditions)

Now you will take your preliminary marketing list including all your legal paperwork plus your facts and features data sheets, and create the best property information worksheet that you can possibly design. Let's build it!

Get yourself a notepad and gather the following information:

What special features does this property have? Gourmet kitchen with spectacular mountain view, garden tub, home office, hardwood floors, tile throughout, in-ground pool, game room, new roof, appliances, carpet and paint, extra storage, sunken living room, fireplace, fruit trees, circle drive, fenced yard? What is special about this property? Write it down. Why did you buy it? What did you like?

Describe everything that will remain with the property as part of the sale, such as draperies/window dressings, ceiling fans, chandeliers, vanities, shelving, appliances, garden equipment, sheds, garage door opener w/remotes, outdoor ornamentals, and so forth. Also make it very clear what will not be included with the sale.

Include all high-energy efficiency-rated materials related to the property. These can include gas appliances that stay, added insulation, a new hot water heater, new windows, solar energy panels, heat pumps, five-star energy-rating certificates, and even shade trees.

Write down area facts, such as parks and recreation areas, shopping centers, transportation lines, locations of schools, hospitals, churches, police, and fire.

Now you will take your preliminary marketing list, including all your legal paperwork plus your facts and features data sheets, and create the best property information worksheet you can possibly design.

Write the following information down, in order, so your ad begins to take shape:

- Begin by taking plenty of digital color photos of the property inside and out on a sunny day and save them in a photo file on your computer to upload and print later.
- Write the street address plus the legal description lot and block (from your deed).
- Write the number of bedrooms, bathrooms, and garage or carport size.
- Write the year built, style (ranch, contemporary, colonial, Tudor, Victorian, Cape Cod, condo, two-story, etc.), size and square footage of living areas including garage and porches.
- Note the type of foundation (slab, block, or pilings), what type of construction (block or wood frame), and type of siding, roof, and heating and cooling.
- List all of the special features.
- List the amenities.
- If your friendly appraiser gave you a high number of, say $200,000, try to list your sales price just below that appraised value and say, "Selling below appraised value @ $199,888.
- List your phone number so you can schedule appointments.
- Make 100 to 150 copies of your facts and features sheets, disclosures, blank contracts, and anything else you would like to provide. These go in the information tubes on your signs. They will also be handed out on open house day and mailed to neighbors and anyone else who might be interested.

Audrie has a nice tool with which to create your facts and features sheet at **www.audrie.com/Flyer_creation.htm**.

(Note: It helps to have an "above average" appraiser's opinion of value. Appraisers don't let on to this—they may even deny it exists—but the word is "puff." This is an amount usually about 6 percent above the actual opinion of value. Sellers on average tack on 6 to 10 percent to the actual price that they expect to get as bargain margin. Again this is added with the expectation that it will be negotiated away by the buyers, thus allowing them to feel as though they got a bargain, nobody admits it exists but you may mention this to your own appraiser, letting him or her know that it will be bargained away. It's controversial, however you do end up selling only for what buyers will pay and that could very well be a newly established higher market price.)

Now is a good time to write your newspaper ad, while the information is fresh in your head and right in front of you. Basically, you need to abbreviate what the information sheet just detailed into a classified ad. When you call the advertising department, they will help you fine-tune your ad. Internet ads and neighborhood flyers can be the entire facts and features sheet, which you can also post on local bulletin boards.

Kevin Wood of **www.byowner.com** says by putting your price and location first, you tend to grab the attention of people who are looking in your price range and area. When advertising in your local area papers you will want to set your open house dates in those ads. Usually Saturday or Sunday from noon until 4:00 P.M. works best, allowing prospective buyers plenty of time to fully investigate the property and documentation. Scheduling it from, say, 1:00 to 2:00 creates an auction atmosphere since all interested parties will be there at the same time. It also gives you the opportunity to bring a lender in since most people are more apt to be willing to sit for an hour, rather than four. Be sure to pay attention to special events that might conflict with your open house date. For instance, no one is likely to show up on Super Bowl Sunday.

Always have no fewer than two people present during an open house and put all valuables in a secure place. Most people are honest—let's keep it that way. Put away all breakables. Candles make good scents; cookies and cider are a nice touch. Soft music tuned low throughout the house is also nice.

Before your showing date arrives, make sure you have yard signs with facts sheets inside a water-resistant holder, and all street corner signs and arrows posted at appropriate locations, intersections included. Check with the local homeowner's association on any restrictions. I recommend a professional sign preferably made of wood that will swing in your front yard. Here's an example of what information to include:

For Sale by Owner
90210 Glenview Oaks Dr.
$199,888 call 555-1212
www.ourhome.com
Shown by appt only

Okay, Fiz, we have a pretty good ad written, the house is tweaked to perfection, and we have all the paperwork necessary to move ahead confidently, so let's go get our buyers.

LIST YOUR HOME FOR FREE OR LOW COST
www.homeportfoliojunction.com (free)
www.allthelistings.com (free; also forms)
www.fsbobasics.com (free)
www.ired.com (free ads and articles)
www.USHX.com (free)
www.homesalewizard.com (free)
www.homewelcome.com (free)
www.homesalediy.com (free)
www.us-real-estate.net (free)
www.onlinerealtysales.com (free)
www.freehomelistings.com (free)
www.gonehome.com/advertise.jsp (free)
www.fsbo-home.com (free plus guide)
www.10realty.com (free plus guide)

continued . . .

www.nuwaymls.com (free or paid MLS)
www.FSBOFreedom.com (30 days free)
www.mlshub.com (free)
www.fsbosystems.com (free plus broker $995 flat free)
www.isoldmyhouse.com (free fill able contracts) good
www.homesbyowner.com (low fee)
www.sellitbyowner.com (low fee)
www.bool.com (low fee)
www.fsboadvertisingservice.com (low fee)
www.sellyourhomeyourself.com (low fee)
www.sellmyhome.com (low fee)
www.fsbo.com (low fee)
www.fisbos.com (low fee)
www.by-owner-ol.com (low fee)
www.privatehomes4sale.com (low fee)
www.forsalebyowner.com (low fee)
www.fsbon.com (low fee)
www.usa4salebyowner.com (low fee)
www.owners.com (low fee, largest inventory)
www.usa.homesalez.com (low fee)
www.buyowner.com (high exposure, not cheap)
www.byowner.com (offers good value)
www.openhousefree.com (open house day)
www.fsbo.net (view listings; for buyers)
www.dmoz.org/Shopping/Classifieds/Homes - FSBO/
www.linkre.com/index.php?t=sub_pages&cat=6462

Holy smokes, Fig! I could almost drown in that stream of potential exposure. Don't worry, my friend; just select your state as if you were looking to buy and see who would give you the best exposure. You certainly don't have to use them all!

Just so you know, Fiz, here's a quick fact: In 1995 2 percent of buyers used the Internet in their search for a home. Today that figure is approaching 75 percent. Odds are pretty good they'll find you when you use any of the services above.

● Let the Negotiations Begin

Fiz, I want to tell you something before we begin: All the horror stories and nightmare scenarios you may have heard in the past regarding deals gone bad or falling through and costing people fortunes in time, money, aggravation, frustration, and lost opportunity more often than not resulted from a lack of proper preparation. The reason people fail to achieve what you are about to do is because they lack the organized information, resources, and proper support structures that are required in order to believe they can do it.

You have been well prepared, my friend! You are also well organized and have plenty of support. In a moment, we are going to execute our strategy according to plan and as you will soon see, the elements that have been put into place up to this point are what will allow you to accomplish your goal in a most effective manner.

● Psychology 101: Reading Your Buyer's Mind

The general rule of negotiation is the party who has the most power wins. That power often comes in the form of superior skill, knowledge, information, strategy, brute strength or resolve, resources, support, planning, organization, and a unique ability to execute. All winning professional sports teams exemplify these attributes according to the degree of confidence they have in using these powers effectively to achieve their goals.

Magic Bullet: When you seek to give people power you have, they will actively try to help you give it to them.

Negotiation, as defined in the dictionary, is "a conferring, discussing, or bargaining to reach agreement." We may also say to transact, haggle, barter, cope, handle, deal with, or manage. Let's say negotiation is a basic means of getting what we want from other people. The ultimate solution is to let other people believe your ideas are their own. If you can achieve that, it only stands to reason there can't be any arguments as the result.

In real estate, the person who appears most desperate will, in most cases, lose the advantage in negotiation. That explains why every real estate buyer looks for motivated sellers, as it naturally builds in advantages to the buyer's benefit. Sellers who can wait to get their price effectively reverse this process or at the very least defend against it. In this case, time really is money!

Your first decision then is based on time. Let's assume the appraised value of the house is $183,500. (Note: A quick way to figure percentages is to divide by 100. $199,888 divided by 100 equals $1,998.88 per percent point or roughly $2,000 for all intents and purposes.)

Start high and test the market at $199,888, or about 9 percent above market. Using this strategy takes time because of the resistance it creates. Buyers will investigate all other competing properties to compare, justify, disqualify, or formulate a counter offer based on what they deem fair in the market.

If they present an offer at 6 percent below your asking price, which is the national average of discounts given by sellers, then that is an offer of about $188,000. This is ideal as you are getting a 3 percent premium above other similar homes in the neighborhood and not paying a commission to do it. Buyers realize other homes have a 6 percent junk fee attached and have not been prepared nearly as well for a fast and trouble-free transfer and will pay for the convenience speed and security you are offering at this price.

Two to three weeks of exposure at this price point will be enough to tell you if you need to go to the next lower level.

The time it takes to sell at market value is based on supply and demand; you can call any real estate office and ask them what the average marketing time for a fairly priced home in your neighborhood is to get a good estimate of how long it takes to find buyers. This could be one day with multiple offers in hot seller's markets, or one, three, or even six months in severely depressed buyers markets. Get to know the market!

If you price your home at or near the same price as competing properties in the market, your benefits package compared to the competing properties will outweigh all the others and your home will be sold to an astute buyer who understands its value relative to all other comparable properties available.

Even if you sell below the appraised value of $183,500 and sell at $179,900 while not paying a 6 percent commission of $11,010, you're still better off than your competition who would get $183,500 - $11,010 = $172,490. Even deducting your benefits package costs of $1,850 from $179,900 still leaves you $178,050—$5,560 better off than your competition.

At this below-market price you would have to concede nothing in negotiation and the property would be disposed of in very short order. You should never have to resort to this type of sales event, but things do happen so you have this option.

Once the initial hurdle of setting and testing the price is done, we'll earn this premium by doing a superior job when it comes to showing the home and answering every question to our buyer's complete satisfaction. Now it's time to screen our market participants—better known as the potential buyer's pool.

● Screening Potential Buyers

Fiz, remember that everything up to this point was done to make the next step easier. You have all the *power* you need to call the shots; you're simply looking for the right buyer to transfer this *power* too. Our real mission is finding the person who wants the *power* you are offering. We are looking for the perfect fit!

Your first requirement of a potential buyer is to determine at the very beginning whether or not they are actually qualified to buy what you are selling. This includes their primary motivations, current situation, time lines, and financial ability to assume control. We will start with their ability to pay because without that, nothing else matters.

Find out if the person is *prequalified*. This is a person who has already spoken with a lender and has a letter stating a certain dollar amount he or she can spend on housing. This is based on a preliminary review of credit standing through credit reports, employment status (pay stubs), two to three years of previous tax returns w/schedules and W2 forms, three months of bank statements verifying funds on hand, and any and all outstanding debt in all forms that they are currently obligated to pay.

If the buyer is *preapproved*, this is basically the gold stamp of approval. It is as direct an endorsement as one can get without actually having a home picked out, appraised, and inspected. This stronger form of proof really says "we, the lenders, have reviewed income, credit history, job stability, cash on hand, and the overall security of the individuals in possession of this letter and we consider them qualified to buy a home up to the stated loan amount on this document. If they like it and the home is found to be of sound quality, value, and title, we will underwrite this loan as agreed. We *trust* them and have no *fear*."

You, the seller, again are in the position of power and as such will not show or negotiate with anyone who hasn't at least obtained prequalification. You can determine this by following a script of sorts. Fiz, before I give you the magic script, you must understand the types of people who appear as buyers or the script will not work.

Understanding Buyers and Human Dynamics

Following are primary character traits:

● Friendly: kind, trusting, amicable, cordial, well disposed
● Introverted: withdrawn, shy, quite, anti-social
● Suspicious: untrustworthy, questionable, doubtful
● Hostile: opposing, fighting, battling, disagreeable
● Factual: literal, exact, correct, discerning, direct
● Extroverted: outgoing, sociable, talkative, high energy
● Reasonable: sensible, credible, probable, intelligent, sound

F.I.S.H.F.E.R. Remember, Fiz, what you are fishing for and cast the right bait. And keep in mind that federal fair housing laws prohibit you from discriminating based on race, color, religion, sex, national origin, disability, or familial status.

Here is your first test, Fiz. See if you can choose who would most likely be the ideal type buyer for your home; if you answer correctly, you get to use the script!

Low ballers: These are usually sophisticated bottom feeders or professional investors who could care less about paying fair market value for anything. Their motivation is greed and they will almost always tell you that you're asking too much. Show or inform them of the appraisal and they will disappear quicker than David Copperfield at a televised event.

Nitpickers: These types will nickel and dime you to death; they will eat up valuable time and criticize all manner of things. They rarely pay fair market value and pull stunts like finding fictitious things wrong on the 24-hour prior to closing walk-through to get you to lower the price in some way. Show them the home's thorough inspection report and home warranty and move on.

Over-protected: These people are a fearful lot; they tend to be *afraid* of everything and ill prepared for anything. They will use escape clauses and contingency planning to avoid getting short changed at a Kool-Aid stand. You can overcome their *fears* if you take the time to quell those *fears*. They may, in fact, be excellent buyers because of your preparation and *fear* removal efforts.

First-time buyers: I encourage you to give these people a listen; they may be well qualified with excellent credit but unaware of the fact that you are only showing the property to pre-qualified and/or approved buyers. Send them off to a neighborhood lender to begin qualifying, while you continue to show the home.

The all-cash buyer: All preapproved buyers are considered to be in a position to pay all cash; the lender is going to give it to you in the form of a closing check. Treat them no differently than a preapproved prospect.

The thief, wannabe, and looker: Disqualify them over the phone, if possible. If they appear at an open house, follow them around every second while asking them 101 qualifying questions. They will soon scurry out the door like the rats they are!

Real estate agents: They *will* call you. Tell them you are working with another agent and you don't feel it would be ethical to speak with them at this time. Do ask them for their card if they appear at your open house and keep it handy; if you ever need an agent chances are you just met a go-getter! If you allow them to bring you a buyer, then say goodbye to 2 to 3 percent of your hard-earned money—or about $5,000 on a $183,500 sale. They are also well-seasoned negotiators and tend to alter your well-laid plans to *their* clients benefit.

Reasonable, preapproved, and motivated inquirer: This is someone who is motivated, has done their homework, has a need for what you have, and wants to see it.

Another smart thing you can do before accepting calls and visitors is to stop by a local lender and have them prepare a few different financing options regarding the purchase of your home. By telling them that you will be sending all prospective buyers who need to be approved their way, they will calculate a few different options with monthly payment amounts, which will help you determine a buyers' capacity to afford your home.

A quick base line to use is that one third of a buyer's monthly income is the limit of what can reasonably be used to pay a mortgage. If the buyer makes $5,000 a month total household income and doesn't have extreme debt, he or she should be able to pay one-third of that, or $1,666.66, a month toward principle, interest, taxes, and insurance (the house payment) without defaulting. Once again, our dear lady Audrie is here to save the day at **www.audrie.com/qualifying_buyers.html**. You just gotta love her, Fiz!

Remember Fiz, you are a do-it-yourself kind of seller. That means you are the one who has to ask the personal questions and they can be tough. But if someone is truly motivated and qualified, he or she will be more than willing to answer these questions in order to move on with the buying process. When people start choking and balking and getting defensive, that is your cue to look at our character list above and take the appropriate action.

Always remain calm, cool, and collected. You are in control and prepared. You might also consider having the following items at your disposal:

● An answering machine or voicemail message that provides basic information related to the home, such as price, location, special features, and Web site. Additionally, prospective buyers can be asked to leave a message. Listening to their message gives you the opportunity to assess the caller's intonation, disposition, and any background sounds. Happy, mad, sad, sour, slow, excited, alert, motivated, scared, cautious, timid, curt—get a feel for their personalities!

● A telephone log helps you keep track of names and phone numbers, and also provides a place to jot down information gathered from using the script. Tape a calendar inside the cover to schedule appointments and monitor other dates of importance.

● Having facts and features sheets by the phone allows you to refer to them easily to give the information being requested.

● Keep all your documents near the phone so you can answer callers' questions quickly.

The following questions may be asked in any order. I have them in the order I would generally begin asking them, but as your conversation takes different paths you will find yourself skipping around and asking various questions as the opportunities arise. Just remember, the more answers you get to as many questions as you can ask without exhausting your prospect, the better. The answers you do get will begin to reveal to you what kind of character type you are dealing with. Print this before you start: **www.maurytome.net/docs/fsbobuyerprofile.doc.**

The Magical Prequalification Script

During your questioning try to emphasize: security, economic well being, a sense of belonging, recognition, and control over one's life. Seek to create a wise, efficient, and mutually beneficial agreement. Empathy is your Magic Bullet!

When the phone rings, or when you choose to call an interested party back, begin with:

● *Hello this is (your first name). May I ask you yours?* Capture the caller's name and phone number through caller ID or by asking. Use the person's name!

● *How did you hear about our home?* Know what advertisement they read so you can add further information to what they already know.

● *Do you currently rent or own?* If they rent, ask, *When will your lease be up?* If they own, ask, *Will you need to sell your present home in order to buy your next one? Is your home currently listed? Do you have a buyer? When is your closing date?*

● *Have you spoken with a lender?* If yes, *Have you been prequalified or preapproved?* If no, *Would you like the name of our local lender?*

● *May I ask why you are moving?*

● *How long have you been looking?*

● *Do you live in the area?* If not, provide area facts and amenities.

● *Will you be buying in the near future?* The response will reveal motivation level.

● *How many homes have you looked at so far?* This will indicate their level of familiarity with the market.

● *When would you ideally like to be settled in?* This will give you an indication of a possible closing date.

● *We will be showing the home this Sunday from noon to 4:00. Would you like to see it then?*

● *Any further questions I can answer for you today?*

This isn't rocket science, Fiz! The simple fact of the matter is, the more questions you ask the more information you have at your disposal to begin to transfer the power as efficiently as possible. You are qualifying them! Stay calm, cool, and collected!

● Final Preparations for Open House Day

Fiz, your home should be ready to go regarding preparation as we thoroughly addressed getting it ready for this event already. We'll just add a few more insights here and then turn you loose on your adoring public.

I myself, Fiz, don't like to be pressured into making a snap decision on the spot without having my facts straight and for that reason I try not to do that to other people (empathy). Yes, it may initially work to get an offer quickly, but that could fall through after things calm down again. I recommend that if you're not desperate to sell, go with the 12 to 4 P.M. time slot.

Use the ad we created earlier and put the words "Open House Sunday 12–4" above it. Your open house advertisement should run Wednesday, Thursday, Friday and Sunday to inform all buyers of Sunday's event and its location. Use Friday and Saturday to deliver facts and features sheets to all your neighbors while inviting them to attend and bring a friend.

You may choose to show the property to certain very hot prospects on days other than scheduled when there are some truly outstanding indications that these are serious buyers who are not going to wait for Sunday.

Make sure your yard signs have facts sheets attached, and all street corner signs and arrows are posted at appropriate locations. In the home, have your facts and features sheets, disclosure sheets, warranties, inspection reports, appraisal, home warranty brochures, blank contracts/offer sheets, earnest money agreements along with all the other information we have collected available and neatly displayed in the order we have gathered them so you'll pick them out effortlessly.

Be sure to have at least one other person present with you and put all valuables in a secure place. Put breakables away, and create a pleasant atmosphere with candles, cookies baking, or cider simmering. Turn on soft music throughout the house. Greet your guests at the door, hand them the facts and features sheets, and invite them in. Don't hover over or follow them around! You may show them a special feature or two and show them the documentation table, but otherwise, let them look around on their own. If they have questions, they will ask.

Some owners of newer homes and manufactured homes received a floor plan of the house. That might be a good addition if it's available. List improvements to the house along with pertinent permits. Include a list of local school (or Web sites where information about local schools can be found). Also, have a guest register. These items can be kept in a three-ring binder in plastic sleeves and left on the counter for the buyers to browse. The information sheet with the picture of the house can be a "take-a-long."

● The Offer

That's it, Fig! You should have an offer on the table in short order, my friend. If you'd like, you may visit **www.dora.state. co.us/real-estate/contracts/contrcts.htm** to see plenty of real estate contracts that you can download for free, these can help you understand the finest of detail if you care to investigate further.

You may also type in ("your state" + real estate contracts) into your **www.google.com** tool bar and hit the "I'm feeling lucky" search key to see what you find in your home state.

Yes, Fiz, I know what kind of feelings are coming over you now so let's get 'em while they're hot! Is it *fear* I hear, Fiz? Are you wondering just how you're going to handle the offer, acceptance, and contract agreement phase of the process? Not to worry, my friend; education is the key! Come with me, let's get it done.

Let's assume the people who bring you an offer probably aren't very knowledgeable about presenting offers and as such are probably going to ask *you* how they're supposed to present it. Fiz, I don't have your specific contract in front of me so I can't really hold your hand here, but if you will do the following things, then once you have an interested buyer, you'll be on your way to the closing table in 45 to 60 days flat. Maybe sooner!

Remember, Fiz, you are in control now; this is where you begin to take hold of your future by believing you can! Lean into the directors' chair and start showing people what to do!

Attach the following or something similar to it, to the contract, earnest money agreement, or offer sheet that you have provided in your home sale package.

> If you would like to make an offer on our home, please indicate the price you are willing to offer along with your full name(s) as you would like them to appear on the title. No earnest money is required at this time. We will reply to your initial offer to inform you of our decision to either accept or offer a counter proposal to your offer within twenty-four to forty-eight hours, if not sooner. If we can come to an initial agreement on price and terms, we will at that time ask that you sit down with us and our attorney to further discuss and finalize our agreements to our mutual satisfaction. Again, you are under no obligation to us in any way by submitting your offer, so please feel free to take your first step in the process of buying this home.

That's telling them what to do!

What do you do if they come back with an offer? What any smart Fiz would do—sit down and give it an initial review! If it's an absurdly low offer, say 20 percent below your asking price, then *reject* it and move on. If it's within 15 percent of your asking price, then I suggest you begin looking at the terms they are asking you to accept so you can formulate a counteroffer. Also remember, Fiz, that we have a partner. We hired that attorney earlier so we could rely on their expertise to conclude this event efficiently.

But before we bother our attorney, we should take into account some of the things that we already have working in our favor along with a couple of those Magic Bullets that we love to use. Let's look at what usually spoils a good contract: contingencies.

Contingencies are often called weasel clauses (*No weasels allowed!*) because some individuals tend to use them to escape or "weasel out of" what appears to be a well-written and binding agreement.

Let's look at some of the more common contingencies that are often standard (boilerplate) language in many preprinted contracts. We'll also take a look at some language that we just don't want in our contract.

- Buyer shall apply for a loan in the amount of $_____ at __% and if said loan cannot be obtained buyer(s) shall be released from further obligation. *If you have a prequalified/preapproved buyer with a letter, then this contingency no longer applies.*

- This offer is contingent upon physical inspection of the property along with a satisfactory report. *You should have arranged your own home inspection followed by the appraisal to find and correct any defects that could become barriers to the sale.*

- This offer is contingent upon a satisfactory appraisal. *If you had your own appraisal done, then you have solid proof that this will not be a major concern. Often you will see additional language here that says:* Buyers are willing to pay "X" amount equal to the offered price, or whichever is less. *That means if the appraisal is less than what they offered they are entitled to buy it at that price! No, Fiz. Change that to read:* If appraised value is lower, sellers may agree to renegotiate. *Now you have a choice to say no or maybe offer a compromise.*

- This offer is contingent upon owner's ability to provide clear title. *Your attorney should have researched this and provided a letter of proof attesting to your ability to provide clear title at closing.*

Those are what can be considered to be standard contingencies in the majority of cases.

Now we have some additional common contingencies that can if not dealt with properly allow the other party to walk away from the deal and also receive their earnest money back!

- This offer is contingent upon buyers' satisfactory inspection of all records and documentation related to the property. *This is open-ended, Fiz; this allows the buyers to nitpick minor details and walk away. (Remember those nitpickers we spoke about?) Your remedy, or defense, is to write "sellers agree to give buyers 48 hours" or whatever you decide, Fiz, to inspect all records and documentation related to the property, if at that time buyers are satisfied, they will initial this paragraph indicating their approval, otherwise they will be released from further negotiations.*

● This offer is contingent upon my partner's and or attorney's approval. *Forty-eight hours, Fiz. You may say, "buyers have 48 hours to obtain any and all approvals required in furthering this agreement, by signing and dating this agreement all participants acknowledge and grant their full approval. Sellers reserve the right to continue to show and retain back-up offers in the event written approvals cannot be obtained."*

● This offer is contingent upon the sale of another specified property. *You really should not allow this, Fiz. Put the burden on the buyer to solve this problem long before they attempt to deal with you! If you choose to allow it, then you may consider increasing the earnest money deposit substantially (to say 10 percent of the sale price, if legal) to insure that buyers will, in fact, sell and be able to qualify by your scheduled closing date or another agreed-upon time.*

● Buyers agree that earnest money in the amount of $_____ will be forfeited by buyers to sellers in consideration of the failure of buyers to fully execute this agreement by date specified here:____.

Buyers also agree that sellers are relieved from all further obligation to buyers or their agents regarding this agreement as a result of buyer's default. *That's an example of a kick-out clause with teeth! I'm not your attorney, Fiz; and this is exactly why you hired one. Attorneys are legally authorized to practice law! You, as a seller, can write this language on your own behalf, but if you screw it up, the buyers' attorney could make you pay.*

● This offer is contingent upon the remaining terms and conditions set forth and agreed to by the contracting parties. *This will cover all other matters that you and the buyers jointly agree must happen. You may agree to pay some of the buyers' closing costs, agree to paint, repair or include certain items, agree to give up possession upon the closing and official title transfer event being recorded, and so forth.*

For all the reasons stated above Fiz, starting with the "contingency" word at the beginning of this discussion, I suggest you put the following statement at the bottom or end of every binding agreement you sign regarding legal contracts:
This entire agreement is subject to my attorney's approval.

Have everyone who is a contracting party to the agreement acknowledge the above statement with their signature. If your attorney disagrees, then they can either accept his or her decision, renegotiate to mutual satisfaction, or walk away—while retaining their good faith earnest money deposit that your attorney is currently holding in trust at that time.

Fact: 40,000 lawsuits are filed each day! They are not all real estate–related, but does that matter?

Now that you have a general idea of how to review an offer looking for any of those weasel clauses, you can begin to formulate just what you are willing to do according to what the buyers have indicated at this point. Are they offering a fair price? Or do you need to counter that by a few percentage points? Are there any conditions they've set forth that just aren't going to work for you? If so, then this is the time to strike them out or draft a statement saying when they must be satisfied, removed, or adjusted according to certain events taking place. Once you have a general outline that you, *the seller alone,* can begin to agree on, that is the time to schedule the appointment with your attorney.

The reason you have said you will return a reply within 24 to 48 hours is so that you have the time necessary to sit down with your attorney and draft a strong counteroffer that satisfies your needs, while hopefully being acceptable to the buyers. If, after the buyers have reviewed your counteroffer and you have what appears to be an initial meeting of the minds or acceptable proposal with only some minor details to be worked out, then set a time quickly to have the buyers meet with you and your attorney to iron out those details and officially set this contract in stone.

Remember, you should be getting top dollar and if this is the case, you can afford to be somewhat generous at this meeting. Don't be greedy!

Don't kid yourself, Fiz, this isn't easy! But if you want to save that commission, slaughter your competition, and get top dollar all at the same time, then you are going to have to work your tail off to get it.

You now have a game plan that removes a fair amount of *fear*, and also gives you the opportunity to achieve new levels of understanding and accomplishment. You can do this! But you cannot drag your feet and run out of time. Start early in the season before the feeding frenzy of buyers floods the market. Smart buyers also think ahead, and they will appear at your door if you present a fair deal. If you find the market telling you it doesn't like your offer, than adjust it accordingly.

You need to believe you can! What you need to do Fiz, is get started! You're going to get plenty of help my friend! Believe me, when you called the cyber-line you tapped a most extraordinary source of power.

Visit with us, my friend, and together we will help others take hold of their own destinies as well. You can find a large family of similarly helpful and truly talented individuals on the Web at your cyberspace home for real estate:

www.magicbullets.com

When you have further questions, my friend, go there, and together we will find the answers.

Your newest friend,

Fig Mentor

GLOSSARY

It was not an easy decision for me as to whether or not I should include a list of terms and definitions. After all, anyone can look these words up in a dictionary. But I felt that by including the definitions of things that can hurt your efforts in real estate, I may save you some grief later.

The following short list of definitions is, to some degree, my own version. My aim is to alert you to the terms, phrases, and situations that can become problematic. I've tried to include a fairly standard definition first, followed by my own slant, where applicable.

Absentee owner/landlord—An owner who does not personally manage or reside at the property owned. What this translates into is less control and ability to manage and repair property properly, which often leads to higher costs and increased frustration.

Acceleration clause/due on sale clause—When you sell, or someone else assumes an interest in your property without your lender's approval, you may be required to pay your loan balance off completely at a given time.

Acts of God—Earthquake, flood, hurricane, lightning, tornado, and so forth. Additional peril insurance is sometimes required if you want protection.

Adjustable rate mortgage—A mortgage loan that allows the interest rate to be changed at specific intervals of the loan's life. This can put additional pressure on you if rates begin to rise.

Adverse possession—A means to acquire title by open, notorious, exclusive, and continuous occupancy of property required by state law. Know your boundary lines and pay attention when others attempt to infringe on your property.

A-frame—A post–World War II house in the shape of an "A." You lose appraisal square footage value and the more angles you use in construction, the more expensive it will be.

Alligator—Requires cash outlays to maintain an investment position that produces no income. For example, raw land and vacant rentals are "animals" that need to be fed.

As is—This means there are no guarantees of condition. You take the risk.

Assessment—The amount of tax or special payment owed to a municipality or association. Always ask if there are any unpaid assessments or if any are projected in the near future.

Attachment—A legal seizure of property to force payment of a debt. Trusts and limited liability corporate structures can protect you here. Seek legal council.

Attractive nuisance—Something that attracts children and can be considered dangerous. For this reason, there are codes that ensure proper fencing is installed around built-in pools.

Balloon mortgage—A debt's major principal balance comes due all at one time. This can create pressure to refinance or sell to pay it off before repossession or foreclosure.

Bankruptcy—The financial inability to pay one's debts when they are due. This affects your credit rating and ability to obtain reasonable credit rates.

Breach of contract—A violation of the terms of a legal agreement. When defaults occur they can be unforeseen and costly. Prudence is not just a girl's name.

Building codes—The minimum standards set by local governments concerning structural, foundations, roofing, plumbing, heating, electrical, safety, sanitation, and others. Code violations are a headache and can be deal breakers; however, they do protect you. Pay attention to code violations when inspecting property.

Caveat emptor—This says, in effect, "Let the buyer beware." And I say, "Beware of the buyer."

Cloud on the title—An outstanding claim or encumbrance that, if valid, will impair the owner's title. Clouds prevent closings as title companies often won't permit transfers without clear title.

Competent parties—Persons legally capable of entering into contract, such as 18 or older, not insane or drunk. You cannot deal with people who can't understand what they do. Your contract can be cancelled as a result.

Condemnation—An involuntary taking of property from an owner for public use. You are compensated but often it is not the amount you feel it is worth.

Conditions/contingencies—Require performance of something in order to proceed in a forward manner of progress. Limit contingency clauses as they create delays and are often used in abusive ways. Satisfy and remove them quickly.

Dead equity—A portion of property that takes up space while contributing no value. You might ask whether or not you are maximizing the cash flow and potential uses of the property.

Default—Failure to fulfill an obligation or promise or failure to perform a specific act or acts.

Defendant—The party being sued in a lawsuit. Always hire competent representation and gather and document as many facts as possible to defend your case effectively.

Disclaimer—A statement whereby responsibility is rejected or denied. Pay attention to disclaimers as they usually aim to take something away from you through small print.

Duress—The act of forcing someone to do something by the use of threats. A court will cancel the agreement as a result.

Easements—Gives others the ability to use and restrict the use of your property for specified purposes. Check for all existing easements when you investigate property. A recent survey along with covenants, deeds, and disclosures should alert you to their existence.

Economic depreciation—A loss of value from all causes outside the property itself. Choose your location wisely as it is a large factor in your property's future value.

Encroachment—If you are being encroached upon, then someone else's building or physical obstruction is intruding on your property. An updated property survey will show this.

Equity of redemption—The right of an owner to recover property that has been foreclosed upon. If you buy foreclosures then you would be wise to know your state's laws regarding redemption.

Estate at sufferance—The wrongful occupancy of property by a tenant after his or her lease has expired. Always review existing leases when evaluating the potential purchase of a property.

Eviction—A costly legal process paid by the landlord to recover possession of his or her property.

Federal fair housing laws—Laws that defend those people who have been discriminated against concerning approval for housing.

Flood plain—Areas that are expected to flood. Insurance can be expensive, if available, and adds no value to an investment.

Foreclosure—The termination of all rights of a mortgagor or the grantee in the property covered by the mortgage. A right of redemption may remain for a period of time if a strict foreclosure rule was not used. Sly investors will sometimes buy these rights and reinstate for themselves.

Forfeiture—You may lose money or something of value if you fail to perform your contract agreements.

Fraud—The use of deception to cause another to suffer a loss. Never use false information. Don't omit material facts when people rely upon them in their decision-making process.

General lien—A debt that may attach to all property owned by the debtor until paid. Defense mechanisms include LLCs and trusts.

Involuntary lien—A debt that may be imposed against property without the owner's consent. Examples include mechanics' liens for work done, assessments, unpaid taxes, IRS judgments, and so forth.

Joint liability—All partners are or can be liable for the entire debt's repayment, not just a prorated share. Limited partnerships are entered into to defend against this possibility.

Laches—Losing your defense by waiting too long or inefficiently asserting your legal right. Document everything in a timely manner if or when violations occur.

Landlocked—Having no access to the property. Easements by prescription or necessity are two ways you may obtain rights of access.

Latent defects—Flaws that are not currently seen that may surface later. Examples are foundation and title problems. Inspect as thoroughly as possible all legal and physical details concerning the property.

Liability—A debt or financial obligation. When you are liable, you are responsible for that debt.

Lien—A charge against property, making it the security for a debt's repayment.

Liquidated damages—Compensation paid to satisfy an agreement for breach of contract.

Lis pendens—A lawsuit pending. Bargain hunters will go to court-houses looking for these notices, since they signal someone has a problem he or she may need help solving.

Maintenance fee—A monthly recurring fee levied by homeowners and condominium associations for common element maintenance. Poor management and collection operations will most often result in higher fees. Ask what is covered by the fee and get a copy of the current operating activity statement.

Management agreement—A binding contract between an owner and someone who agrees to manage. Review these agreements carefully for ambiguous conditions of employment, the fees charged, and the method of proceeds distribution. When you give someone else control you must ensure you have measures in place to control them!

Marginal property—A property that is barely profitable to use or operate. Add management fees, a rising adjustable rate mortgage, and vacancies, and you will have one hungry alligator on your hands.

Moratorium—A period of time where certain things are not permitted, such as no new construction and so forth.

Negative cash flow—Exists when a property owner has to spend more than the amount that is brought in to operate a property.

Nonconforming—Use that violates zoning restrictions but is allowed to remain "grandfathered." Most often, no replacement is granted if it is destroyed.

Notice to quit—A notice to a tenant to vacate a rented property. Proof of delivery can be sent by certified mail, posting on the property, and/or hand delivery. A combination of all three usually drives home the point and covers the bases regarding proper delivery rules.

Obsolescence—Signals a loss in value due to limited use and desirability, mostly affected by age, design, and utility (which are functional), followed by location (which is external).

Oral contracts—Generally not enforceable in the sale of real estate; statute of frauds says the agreement must be in writing. So use a written contract or lose the good deals.

Ordinances—Regulate the use of land in some way. Examples include what you can build, how, and where.

Power of sale clause—Allows lenders to sell your property without court authority if you default. I would go elsewhere if I could not have that clause removed.

Prepayment penalty—Penalty for paying your loan off early. Used more often when interest rates are high to discourage refinancing or early retirement of the loan. Avoid these clauses like the plague!

Private mortgage insurance (PMI)—Protects the lender in the case of the borrower's default. It is generally required when the borrower puts down less than 20 percent of the purchase price and has no other mortgage guarantees. Try to put down 20 percent to avoid PMI. Get creative and avoid this added cost, which contributes no real value in property.

While on the subject of mortgage insurance, don't fall for the mortgage protection policy that pays off your mortgage in case of death. Once again, you're paying for a policy that protects the lender for the most part. In the past, lenders have tried to slip it in. I always decline it. Your situation may differ. The elderly with limited incomes may benefit by it.

Rent control—Laws or ordinances that regulate the amount of rent that can be charged. It is designed to prevent price gouging by unscrupulous landlords. I would not buy rental property within rent-controlled districts, even though it is fair to tenants.

Servient tenant property—Provides a beneficial easement for the use of access to another property. Structure deals with adjoining owners who may grant you an easement right to landlocked parcels of land, then acquire those seemingly worthless properties for a song.

Setbacks—Restrictions that keep you from building too close to property lines. Reasons may be to prevent obstructions of view, to create easement access, to prevent fires from jumping from building to building, and so forth.

Soft market—Generally speaking, when supply exceeds demand; could indicate a buyer's market.

Special assessments—Levies against property to help pay for improvements that benefit the public and as a result, hopefully benefit the property as well.

Specific performance—The court makes you perform your contractual obligations and when justified, you may be forced to comply.

Straw man—One who acts to conceal the identity of the true purchaser of property. A straw man acquires, then transfers the property to another. This may be done to undo a seller's refusal to sell to select individuals or to assemble large parcels of land for large projects, while limiting knowledge to sellers of the need for their land to complete the project.

Sublease—A lease from one tenant to another. You often lose the ability to prudently control events when you allow subleasing— that is, renting your property to others. It is usually highly discouraged and most often, not permitted.

Subordination clause—Lowers your position in lien priority and increases your risk.

Tax—A government charge. Use a CPA and lawyer to limit taxation through maximizing your legal deductions. Create legal tax shelters through rental real estate.

Termites—Insects that bore into wood and destroy it. Don't let them scare you off when investing. Investigate when others run; there is good money in these situations.

Tort—A small infraction that renders the perpetrator liable for damages to the victim.

Trespass—The unlawful entry or possession of another's property. Even as an owner landlord, you must have permission and give notice for general entry of a rented or leased property.

Words on paper don't really strike fear in our minds when they do not apply to our current affairs directly; however, if they become a factor in your quest toward prosperity, you will then notice just how harmful and aggravating these words can be. Simply keep them as watchwords to know and when they appear, your inner voice should alert you to pay them the special attention they deserve. I hope this short list of words never comes back to haunt you. Remember to investigate further when they appear and you'll be okay.

FRIENDS OF OUR FAMILY
INTERNET RESOURCES

There are *no* affiliate links in any of these, they *are* friends!

Search engine: www.Google.com
Second choice: www.Yahoo.com
Third & final: www.vivisimo.com

General Real Estate Top Picks

www.realestateabc.com/top100/top100.asp?Cat=1
(top 100 sites)

www.totalrealestatesolutions.com

www.reals.com

www.realestate4.com

www.linkre.com

www.dealmakerscafe.com

www.propertysites.com

www.relibrary.com

www.LetsDoDeals.com

www.thecreativeinvestor.com

www.UrbanBombs.com *rated PG*

www.homebuyingrealestate.com

www.reidepotshop.com

www.carei.com

Research Sites

www.inman.com *(your must source for news)*

www.meyersgroup.com *(economic news)*

www.fnis.com/Research/index.asp *(latest market news)*

www.fnismarketintelligence.com/2003/03-21/default.asp *(news)*

www.firstamres.com/news/articles.jsp *(analysis)*

www.searchbug.com *(find people, places & things)*

www.usacitylink.com *(relocation guide to cities)*

www.nhfind.com *(community info)*

www.realtytimes.com *(market conditions)*

www.newspaperlinks.com/home.cfm *(electronic newspapers)*

www.bestplaces.net/ *(city and school facts and more)*

www.50states.com *(state facts & info)*

www.census.gov *(statistics of the U.S.)*

www.dataquick.com *(get your data here)*

www.infospace.com *(your phone book and more)*

www.realtor.com *(homes for sale nationwide)*

www.netronline.com/public_records.htm *(public records search)*

www.policyholdersofamerica.org/index2.html *(insurance issues)*

www.kwsnet.com *(scroll to real estate, huge resource)*

www.infocredit.com/ *(background checks)*

www.creditretriever.com *(credit reports on tenants)*

www.FINDTHESELLER.com *(track them down)*

www.policeauctions.com *(auctions)*

www.buyerstrust.com *(buyers agent directory)*

Financial

www.myFICO.com *(get your credit score)*

www.experian.com *888-397-3742*

www.tuc.com *800-888-4213*

www.equifax.com *800-685-1111*

www.bankrate.com *(today's rates and more)*

www.bankrate.com/brm/mortgage-calculator.asp *(calculator)*

www.interest.com *(financial/loans)*

www.eloan.com *(another)*

www.mortgagequotes.com *(another)*

www.quickenmortgage.com *(another)*

www.mortgage-referral.com *(another)*

www.lendingleaders.com *(another)*

www.interest.com/discussion/ *(mortgage discussion)*

www.debtbug.com *(stop foreclosure)*
www.mtgprofessor.com/calculators.htm *(calculator heaven)*
www.cybernetmortgage.com *(calculators/loans Texas)*
www.mortgage101.com *(calculators and more)*
www.algebrahelp.com/calculators/index.htm *(higher math)*
www.homefair.com *(calculators & relocation info)*
www.lendingleaders.com *(finance)*
www.homebuyingguide.com/default.asp
  (4 free finance books) PDF
www.homewarrantyexperts.com *(find a good warranty co.)*
www.orhp.com *(home warrantees)*
www.homeloans.va.gov *(military forms resource)*

Inspection/Appraisal

www.inspectamerica.com *(free inspection reports)*
www.appraisalfoundation.com *(click on ".ORG")*
www.appraisalinstitute.com/default.asp *(find your appraiser)*
www.naifa.com *(find another)*
www.appraisersforum.com/forum/index.php *(ask an appraiser)*
www.electronicappraiser.com *(general valuations)*
www.camerondirect.com/compsources.shtml *(comparable data)*
www.ashi.com *(find a home inspector)*
www.homeinspections.com *(5,000 inspectors)*
www.independentinspectors.org *(ditto)*
www.nachi.org/bbsystem/index.php *(ask a home inspector)*
www.inspectorsjournal.com *(ditto)*

Contracts/Forms Suppliers

www.audrie.com
www.audrie.com/Flyer_creation.htm *(make a flyer)*
www.uslegalforms.com
www.kaktus.com
www.urgentbusinessforms.com
www.standardlegal.net
www.isoldmyhouse.com/forms.html
  (free fill able contracts) excellent!
www.prepaidlegal.com/newCorp/lrc.html
  (free contracts all 50 states)

www.dora.state.co.us/real-estate/contracts/contrcts.htm
(free Colorado contracts)

www.eHow.com *(then follow finance to real estate)*

www.mortgage-investments.com/Real_estate_and_mortgage_
Forms/form_fr.htm *(free)*

www.findlaw.com *(back out of page, pop up allows free access)*

www.alllaw.com/forms/real_estate *(sample forms/ lawyer search)*

www.attorneyfinder.com/index.html *(find an attorney)*

www.attorneylocate.com/index.html *(ditto)*

www.turnpike.net/lawnet *(questions answered free)*

www.homefindersbulletin.com/docs/checklist.pdf
(free tenant move in checklist)

www.thelpa.com/lpa/free-forms.html?id=nyy2upaZ
(free landlord forms)

www.legalscholar.com/links/realestateassociations.html
(law resource)

www.witnessdesigns.com *(wide variety of signage)*

www.webuyhousessigns.com *(supplier of signs)*

Forums & Networking

www.creonline.com *(creative investment)*

www.MRLANDLORD.com *(property mgmt)*

www.thelpa.com/lpa/index.html *(landlord protection)*

www.lease2purchase.com *(networking)*

www.legalscholar.com *(associations)*

www.propertyinvesting.com/forum *(+ cash flow)*

www.camerondirect.com *(clubs)*

www.neodemesne.com *(friend to all)*

www.naked-investor.com *(lease option forum)*

www.creative-financing-solutions.com/hips.html
(20 repair forums)

www.creative-financing-solutions.com/realestate.html
(43 finance forums)

www.realestatelink.net/clubs.html *(clubs & associations)*

www.apartmentassociation.com *(apartment owners associations)*

www.creonline.com/clubs.htm *(real estate clubs nationwide)*

www.reiclub.com *(more clubs)*

www.bhg.com *(ladies discussion, scroll to bottom)*

www.property.com/news.html *(newsgroups & lists)*
www.realestateinvesting.com/investors-associations/search.asp
www.realestatetalks.com/index.php *(R.E. Forum)*
www.newyork.craigslist.org/about/cities.html *(discuss & more)*
www.gladwell.com/tp_excerpt2.html *(networking triggers)*
www.lease2purchase.com/php/letsnetwork/letsnetwork.php
   (do it)

Commercial Investment Club

www.icsc.org *(browse navigation bar)*
www.ree.com *(1031 exchanges)*
www.naeba.org *(exclusive buyers agents)*

Home Improvement

www.hometime.com *(plan your work)*
www.diyonline.com *(remodel it)*
www.doityourself.com *(super site)*
www.build.com *(home plans)*
www.nahb.org *(find a builder under resources)*
www.decoratorsecrets.com *(finishing touches)*
www.plbg.com *(plumbing repair forum)*
www.paintcenter.org/pexpertqa1.cfm *(the world of paint)*
www.forums.gardenweb.com/forums/#subs *(the garden)*

Reverse Directory

www.anywho.com *(reverse lookup)*
www.infospace.com *(multiple directory)*
www.switchboard.com *(find numbers)*
www.people.yahoo.com *(general addresses)*
www.whowhere.lycos.com *(last chance)*

Street-Finders/Maps

www.randmcnally.com
www.mapsonus.com
www.mapquest.com
www.globexplorer.com
www.epa.gov/enviro/html/em/index.html *(E.P.A maps)*
www.fodors.com (travel)

FSBO Sites

www.resultsnow.com
www.directoryrealestate.com
www.topfsbo.com *(top 100 fsbo sites)*
www.mlshub.com/

List Your Home for Free or Low Cost

www.homeportfoliojunction.com *(free, Sue is a doll)*
www.allthelistings.com *(free also forms under resources)*
www.fsbobasics.com *(free)*
www.ired.com *(free ads & articles)*
www.realestatelistingfree.com *(free)*
www.USHX.com *(free)*
www.homesalewizard.com *(free)*
www.homewelcome.com *(free)*
www.homesalediy.com *(free)*
www.us-real-estate.net *(free)*
www.onlinerealtysales.com *(free)*
www.freehomelistings.com *(free)*
www.gonehome.com/advertise.jsp *(free)*
www.aireo.com/propertylistings/index.shtml *(free)*
www.general@realestatelistingfree.com *(free)*
www.fsbo-home.com *(free + guide)*
www.10realty.com *(ditto)*
www.nuwaymls.com *(free or paid MLS)*
www.FSBOFreedom.com *(30 days free)*
www.mlshub.com *(free)*
www.fsbosystems.com *(free + broker $995 flat)*
www.isoldmyhouse.com *(free fill able contracts) good*
www.homesbyowner.com *(low fee)*
www.sellitbyowner.com *(low fee)*
www.bool.com *(low fee)*
www.fsboadvertisingservice.com *(low fee)*
www.sellyourhomeyourself.com *(low fee)*
www.sellmyhome.com *(low fee)*
www.fsbo.com *(low fee)*

www.fisbos.com *(low fee)*
www.by-owner-ol.com *(low fee)*
www.privatehomes4sale.com *(low fee)*
www.forsalebyowner.com *(low fee)*
www.fsbon.com *(low fee)*
www.usa4salebyowner.com *(low fee)*
www.owners.com *(low fee, largest inventory)*
www.usa.homesalez.com *(low fee)*
www.buyowner.com *(high exposure, not cheap)*
www.byowner.com *(Kevin offers good value)*
www.openhousefree.com *(open house day)*
www.fsbo.net *(view listings, for buyers)*
www.ownerwillcarry.com *(a neat twist)*
www.dmoz.org/Shopping/Classifieds/Homes_-_FSBO/
  (want more?)
www.linkre.com/index.php?t=sub_pages&cat=6462
  (that's enough!)

Foreclosure Searches

www.foreclosurefreesearch.com
www.hud.gov
www.homesteps.com
www.fanniemae.com
www.propertydisposal.gsa.gov/property
www.treas.gov/auctions/customs *(auctions)*
www.all-foreclosure.com *(can you guess?)*
www.policeauctions.com *(auctions)*

More Great Sites

www.johntreed.com/realestate.html *(John exposes Gurus)*
www.homeadvisor.com *(Bill Gates does real estate)*
www.kesslerkeystosuccess.com *(wise man)*
www.thomaslucier.com *(Tom teaches)*
www.richardroop.com *(a rich resource)*
www.legalwiz.com/realestatesites.htm *(one smart Bill)*
http://www.wealthaddress.com/Real_Estate_Articles.html
  (article resource)
www.groups.msn.com/RayComosHouseBuyingkindom *(paste it)*

www.resultsnow.com
www.propertyinvesting.com
www.realestatelink.net
www.realestateclub-la.com
www.bizweb.com
www.islandtime.com/surfsup/
www.racelinecentral.com/Monster/monsterlinks1.html
www.homeseekers.com
www.cyberhomes.com
www.homescout.com
www.homeadvisor.com
www.nolo.com *(form your LLC)*
www.realestate.yahoo.com/re/
www.info-s.com/estate.html
www.ecki.com/links/srlst.shtml *(39 more sites)*
www.creonline.com/site-map.html *(article heaven)*
www.thegaryhalbertletter.com
    (marketing genius and friend) rated PG
www.selfstartersweeklytips.com/forum
    (technology answers) Lynn
www.im4newbies.com/forum/index.php
    (more tech support) Mike
www.webproworld.com/forum.php *(programmers) Brittany*
www.216.120.234.168/~totalli/forum
    (go to success forum) Mark
www.mountaineagleweb.com/Creative/Creative.htm *(creativity)*
www.anthonyrobbins.com/community *(self improvement forum)*
www.positive-club.com *(discover your power)*
www.herosoul.com *(be a hero) my good friend Sharif*
www.principledprofits.com *(Shel teaches cooperative effort)*
www.thomaslucier.com/resources.html
    (Didn't find it? Dig deeper)
www.twomen.com *(my recommendation for movers)*

Bring your finds home to the family at:
www.MagicBullets.com *Dan*

INDEX

Give the Gift of
Magic Bullets
in Real Estate
to Your Friends and Colleagues

CHECK YOUR LEADING BOOKSTORE OR ORDER HERE

❏ **YES**, I want _____ copies of *Magic Bullets in Real Estate* at $19.95 each, plus $4.95 shipping per book. (Ohio residents please add $1.25 sales tax per book.) Canadian orders must be accompanied by a postal money order in U.S. funds. Allow 15 days for delivery.

❏ **YES**, I am interested in having Dan Auito speak or give a seminar to my company, association, school, or organization. Please send information.

My check or money order for $_____ is enclosed.

Please charge my: ❏ Visa ❏ MasterCard
❏ Discover ❏ American Express

Name _____

Organization _____

Address _____

City/State/Zip _____

Phone_____ E-mail _____

Card # _____

Exp. Date_____ Signature _____

Please make your check payable and return to:
BookMasters, Inc. ● P.O. Box 388, Ashland, OH 44805

Call all credit card orders to: 800-247-6553
fax 419-281-6883 ● order@bookmasters.com
www.atlasbooks.com

You may also send a check or money order to:
Hathshire Press ● 1619 Three Sisters Way, Kodiak, AK 99615
www.MagicBullets.com www.HathshirePress.com

Recd from Amazon.Ca on May 18/05
Cost : $ 17 $\frac{58}{}$